FLYIN' FLOYD

The Unvarnished Biography of an American Dirt Racing Legend

David M. McGee

Jan-Carol
Publishing, Inc
"every story needs a book"

FLYIN' FLOYD:
The Unvarnished Biography
of an American Dirt Racing Legend
Written by David M. McGee

Published May 2019
Little Creek Books
Imprint of Jan-Carol Publishing, Inc.

ISBN: 978-1-950895-50-2
Library of Congress Control Number: 2019939694

You may contact the publisher:
Jan-Carol Publishing, Inc.
PO Box 701
Johnson City, TN 37605
publisher@jancarolpublishing.com
jancarolpublishing.com

Table of Contents

Acknowledgments

This book began as a simple effort to pay tribute to one of the greatest drivers I ever saw behind the wheel of a race car. Somewhere along the way it evolved into a year-long treasure hunt, chasing down decades-old results and photos as well as trying to jog people's memories about events of a half-century ago.

In the end, it was an absolute joy and labor of love to produce, largely due to sharing the journey with folks who embraced my quest to recount this story as fully and accurately as possible.

The task would have been nearly impossible without three people: J.T. LeFever, Michael LeFevers, and Bob Markos.

First and foremost, my deepest appreciation to J.T., who had the great sense to conduct a lengthy, detailed interview with Flyin' Floyd years ago and generously allowed me to utilize parts of it to better bring Floyd's voice into this project. He also shared countless stories and images from his remarkable DirtFans.com website.

A huge thank you to Michael LeFevers and the people at the Fremont, Ohio Speedway Hall of Fame who rescued and shared the priceless photographic archives of the now-defunct *Mid-American Auto Racing News*. Those wonderful images surely tell this story more richly.

This project was helped greatly by the contributions of Bob Markos, the historian of the National Dirt Late Model Hall of Fame, who served as a sounding board and provided essential information along with several unique photographs—and who consistently cheered me on.

Finding photographs was surprisingly challenging, but thanks to

John Butler, Greg Courtney, Paula Gilbert, Eric Nickelson, Brian Norton, Eddie Roche, and Steve Struve for sharing images, and to photographers like Butler, Steve Cottle, Raymond Kelley, Ray Rogers, Steve Struve, and Ernest Thomas who braved heat, cold and long hours to document those races.

Mere words cannot describe how proud I am to include the incredible artwork of Roger Warrick in this project. Roger's caricature of Floyd perfectly captures his career highlight World 100 victory, the mighty Duncan Chevelle, and the backstory of that day, including Floyd's fourth Glen Este title.

Thank you to Floyd's family, who initially thought too few would remember him; thank you for sharing this amazing man with his fans for all those years.

A highlight for me was tracking down John Butler and Carroll Hamilton, who teamed up to profile Floyd in words and photos in *Stock Car Racing* magazine in 1975. John was especially gracious to allow access to his timeless 1973 World 100 negatives.

Thank you to all my other heroes as well: drivers and car owners who shared their best memories and stories. I so appreciate the chance to speak with Morgan Chandler, William "Fats" Coffey, Rodney Combs, Roger Grossnickle, Tom Helfrich, Larry Moore, Gary Rice, and E.M. Snowden Jr.

Many, many folks provided names, contact information, details, suggestions, and encouragement as I raced down Memory Lane against Father Time. Thank you to Shirley Briscoe, Gary Brock, John Campbell, Randy Crump, James Crump, Angelia Kelley-Dickerson, Anthony Goodpaster, Brad Greer, Drew Hierwarter, Will Holleran, Tom Lesshaft, Ericka Napier, Gary Parker, Charles Poindexter, Shane Ruth, Patti Schiller, Win Smith, Penny Snowden, Joe Tennis, Jerry Wahl, Nelson Wierenga, and Ed Woodward. I'd like to add a very special mention of the late Mike Roland, who encouraged me to pursue this project years ago, but sadly didn't live to see it completed.

Thank you to the sports writers and track publicists who cranked out results stories and information recovered decades later from the pages of the *Anderson Herald* (IN), *Bloomington Pantagraph* (IL), *Cincinnati Enquirer* (OH), *Circleville Herald* (OH), *Clay City Times* (KY), *Danville Advocate-Messenger* (KY), *Greensburg Daily News* (IN), *Hamilton News Journal* (OH), *Jackson County Banner* (IN), *Logan Daily News* (OH), *Louisville Courier Journal* (KY), *Mansfield News Journal* (OH), *Mid-American Auto Racing News* (OH), *Muncie Star Press* (IN), *Nashville Tennessean* (TN), *Pensacola News Journal* (FL), *Piqua Daily Call* (OH), *Richmond Palladium-Item* (IN), *Rushville Republican* (IN), *Seymour Tribune* (IN), and *Tampa Tribune* (FL).

A multitude of details came from those stories, unearthed through countless searches on Newspapers.com. Another great resource was the UltimateRacingHistory.com website.

This book was written during a time when my girlfriend, Debbie Helton, was facing down cancer for the umpteenth time. The work provided a temporary haven, a chance to slip back in time to simpler, more carefree days. I thank God she is doing well now.

I dedicate this work to the memory of my late father Fred McGee, who indulged my youthful enthusiasm for auto racing and drove countless miles to race tracks oh so many years ago. Going racing was our time and allowed us to share some great moments. I miss him terribly.

Introduction

B efore reading further, please take a moment to study the main photograph on this book's cover, for it says much about this story. At its center is the bearded, unsmiling face of Floyd Gilbert, age 44 at that moment, clenching the checkered flag from another victory on a Kentucky dirt oval. Why isn't he smiling? He's accomplished his job: winning. The man was relentless in his pursuit of victory. As determined as they come, Floyd was fond of saying, "I didn't come to run second."

Look closely at the car, the vaunted Duncan's Delight Chevelle—among that era's best prepared dirt late model racers. R.L. Duncan, the owner of a heavy equipment moving business in Lexington, Kentucky, had two full-time employees looking after his race cars. Brothers Logan and Charles Grider were top-notch mechanics and innovators who kept the big red machine in top condition.

While the car was doubtlessly spotless when it rolled off the transporter earlier that evening, in the photo it is spattered with red clay across the sheet metal and covering most everything inside the cockpit, the dirt easily penetrating the wire screen that replaced the windshield. Dirt tracks, especially Kentucky dirt tracks, were Floyd's playground.

Examine the creases, scratches, and dents on that steel door. This was the era before lightweight fabricated race cars with composite body panels. The car was lettered as Chevelle because that's what it was; on-track contact had wrinkled the sheet metal.

Notice the square steel rub rail near the bottom door seam, which afforded a bit of protection when rivals ran too close or tempers overheated.

And there is the checkered flag, gripped tightly in Gilbert's left hand—like so many others from oval tracks across his native Ohio, central Kentucky, Indiana, Michigan, Georgia, Florida, and points in between. In all, Gilbert registered some 500 feature race wins, many against the greatest drivers of two generations of late model racing: Larry Moore, Gene Petro, Billy Teegarden, Butterball Woodridge, Tom Helfrich, Charlie Swartz, William "Fats" Coffey, Eddie Carrier, and David Speer, National Dirt Late Model Hall of Famers all.

Gilbert was old school, a throwback before such things were popular. He came from "junkers," and boldly raced the hair-raising figure-eight class before earning stardom in steel-bodied late models.

Stock Car Racing magazine proclaimed Gilbert the "king of Midwestern dirt track racing," and "master of the dirt." In a 1975 profile, J.T. LeFever's "DirtFans.com" website—dedicated to preserving dirt racing history—resurrected the "Master of the Dirt" title for its story about Floyd.

He had to be.

In 1970, Gilbert turned in his union card and walked away from steady paychecks to race professionally on the hard-scrabble dirt ovals around his southern Ohio home. One night at Kentucky's Clay City Raceway, he succinctly summarized his nomadic existence of chasing checkered flags after leading the first 68 circuits of a 100-lap race until the engine blew.

"Some weeks you eat steak; some weeks you eat bologna," Gilbert said to a wide-eyed 14-year-old fan who'd made his way over to the pit area to offer condolences on what would be the team's only 1972 loss at Clay City, and one of just a handful that season.

I was that teenager and, at that time, maybe the biggest Floyd Gilbert fan around. Three years later, while still in high school, I began covering the racing action at Clay City and other tracks for local newspapers and the long-forgotten Cincinnati-based racing publication *OKI Racing News*.

Old-timers—one of which I now apparently am—love to romanticize the era, claiming the primarily homebuilt cars were the most appealing, the drivers the most courageous, and that races were won by equal parts skill and determination.

Through college I disconnected from dirt racing as new opportunities shifted my focus to drag racing and NASCAR. One day, on a trip home to Kentucky, I picked up a copy of the December 2004 issue of *Stock Car Racing* magazine. There on page 57 was a photo of Floyd—wearing sunglasses, a plaid shirt, ball cap, and suspenders—being inducted into the National Dirt Late Model Hall of Fame. An enormous smile crept across my face.

Floyd took his earthly checkered flag May 25, 2010, but his legacy lives on.

Come along as we revisit simpler times, when steel late models wore paint and hand-painted numbers and were driven by daring men who raced for both the challenge and the payday.

CHAPTER 1:

Some Weeks You Eat Steak

A solitary figure walked slowly yet purposefully along the edge of the saturated reddish-brown clay surface while a mud-spattered truck lumbered by, spraying a seemingly futile stream of water as the relentless, late summer sun beamed down.

Dust-covered speakers clinging to aging, creosote-dipped wooden posts relayed the familiar country refrain of Sammi's Smith's "Help Me Make It Through the Night," a tune with a title that seemed appropriate, given the high-speed hijinks about to unfold.

While most in the nearby tree-lined pit area busied themselves changing tires, tuning engines, or otherwise working on a colorful collection of cars, the solitary man continued walking—slightly stooped over with his hands behind his back, peering downward through dark aviator sunglasses as if he'd lost something.

He had thick, black hair and his distinctive face was framed by an Abraham Lincoln beard. He was already dressed for work in boots, black jeans with a worn red shop rag hanging from the back pocket, and a weathered red windbreaker with a white stripe on the right side, decorated with Kendall GT-1 Racing Oil patches on the left and back.

Neither the passing water truck nor the song broke the man's concentration. His was a deliberate stride, observing and filing away information much like the ground beneath his boots absorbed water. His

1

photographic memory intently cataloging how water soaked into the porous surface as he tried to visualize where traction would somehow magically appear later, once the quagmire dried out.

As the sun began its lazy decent into the western horizon, the call went out for drivers to begin packing the track. It was time to go to work.

This was the summer of 1972 and "Flyin' Floyd" Gilbert—the solemn man who examined every pore, rut, and blemish in the racing surface—was accomplishing something utterly extraordinary in the world of dirt late model stock car racing: winning 42 feature races in just 53 starts driving a Chevelle masterfully prepared by car builder and owner Morgan Chandler—a win rate of 80%. Seven wins in other cars brought his total to 49 wins in 65 races.

Gilbert's win total that season was the most in the U.S. on dirt and might easily have been the most in the nation, had Dick Trickle not collected 67 victories on paved Midwestern ovals: an impressive total, but one requiring more than a hundred starts.

Perhaps nowhere was Gilbert and Chandler's success more evident than at Kentucky's Clay City Raceway, a high-banked, high-speed, half-mile that saw them capture the checkered flag in ten of eleven feature starts, nearly a fourth of all that season's wins.

Carved into Red River bottomland where Kentucky's mountains meet the rolling bluegrass region, Clay City demanded the utmost from man and machine. Success required horsepower—much like the adjoining drag strip—and the nerve to drive a car deep into the first and third turns, breathing the throttle, and then matting the gas and powering off the corners.

"I liked those long straightaways," Chandler said decades later. "And the track didn't get hard and slick like so many others."

With 750 horsepower and tons of torque beneath his right foot, it would be easy to drive too far into the corner and wrestle the steering wheel for control. Lift early, and you open the door for the next driver in line. Get back to the throttle too soon, and the result was usually a spinout—too late and the car behind you would zip by.

Seeing Gilbert wheel that car at Clay City was to witness art in motion.

After rocketing down the straightaway, Gilbert would momentarily lift his right foot from the throttle and the flame of unburned fuel would belch from the car's exhaust, exiting behind the driver and in front of the rear tires just as he threw the 3,500-pound beast into the corner. When Gilbert's right foot went back down, the dual Holley carburetors bulging through the gold metalflake hood would suck in fuel and air, the 520-cubic inch powerplant would roar, and the golden chariot seemed to explode off the corner and down the straightaway.

"I like running down there in that part of Kentucky," Gilbert told *Cincinnati Enquirer* sports writer Webb Mathews that summer. "The people are unequaled in the way they treat you."

Perhaps the most amazing aspect was that Floyd's wins came while competing against the very best of that generation of dirt stars. The 1970s racing circuit stretching across central Kentucky, Ohio, and Indiana boasted no less than twenty drivers whose names would ultimately be enshrined in the National Dirt Late Model Hall of Fame, and another dozen capable of winning on any given weekend.

Legendary names like Eddie Carrier Sr., William "Fats" Coffey, Delmas Conley, Bruce Gould, Tom Helfrich, Ralph Latham, Vern LeFevers, Chuck McWilliams, Larry Moore, Pat Patrick, Gene Petro, David Speer, Charlie Swartz, Billy Teegarden, and Paul "Butterball" Woodridge raced alongside Gilbert during his storied career, yet he still tallied some 500 victories and 16 track championships.

It would be easy to argue Floyd could have many more wins racing against lesser foes, but it was competition that drove Gilbert. He was 42 years old in 1972, having already raced cars for two decades. His prime—along with top-shelf equipment—arrived very late in his career, but he took full advantage of those opportunities.

The race on this night, the start of Labor Day weekend, meant the midwestern racing season was winding down. Yet Floyd's mind was focused on redemption. The night's 50-lap feature paid $1,000 to the winner, more than twice the normal payout for the regular 40-lapper—the same amount he'd let slip through his fingers a few weeks before.

Floyd Gilbert (No. 28) leads rival Paul "Butterball" Wooldridge (No. 59) in the Duncan's Delight Chevelle at Kentucky's Clay City Raceway in 1972 where Gilbert won ten of 11 features. (Photo by Steve Cottle, courtesy Fremont Hall of Fame, Mid-American Auto Racing News archives)

Back on July 21, Gilbert was the fastest qualifier—just like nearly every other week. He'd led the first 68 circuits of Clay City's 100-lap Mid-Season Championship race before an engine failure sent him to the pits. Rival Butterball Wooldridge capitalized on his misfortune and claimed the top prize, driving the familiar red Chevelle owned by Lexington, Kentucky's R.L. Duncan.

This $1,000 could help Gilbert pay some bills, put fuel in his motorhome so he could spend the winter racing in Florida, and add a few extra cans of Hudepohl to the cooler.

There was also some extra incentive; promoter John Kennon had posted a $100 bounty for anyone who could beat Gilbert that evening. While their winning streak was good for Gilbert and Chandler's bank accounts, their domination dampened the suspense spectators crave, and attendance slumped. They were that unbeatable.

Although the pits were filled with talent from four states, Gilbert quickly served notice that he would once again be difficult to handle. After the track was packed and the call went out for qualifying, Gilbert was first to line up along the grassy path in front of the track's white, two-story, cinderblock control tower. His single lap around the half-mile was clocked at 23.6 seconds, for an average speed of 76 miles per hour—just enough to be the fastest qualifier. While nowhere close to his 22.10-second record pace, the big Chevelle still topped 100 miles per hour down the track's long straightaways.

Others who were fast on the stopwatch that night were Ohioan Jim Patrick; Indiana native Tommy Day, driving the always dangerous Ruth Motors Chevelle; Kentucky stars Baldy McLaren; a young Charlie Swartz aboard his 8-Ball Chevelle; central Kentucky speed merchants E.M. Snowden Jr., and Ray Cash; along with West Virginia fan favorite Tudy Adkins.

Gilbert, Day, Cash, and McLaren comprised the four-car fast dash, a four-lap preliminary won handily by Gilbert. In a preview of the night's feature, Gilbert also won the ten-lap heat race featuring the night's fastest qualifiers.

In the 50-lap feature race, McLaren started on the outside of the front row and led the first lap in the No. 195 Chevelle, owned by Wilburn Burnett. But on the second circuit, Gilbert spurred Chandler's gold Chevelle into the lead as the pack charged down the backstretch.

Day brought out the night's first caution on lap four, spoiling his debut for Lloyd Ruth by hitting the front-stretch guardrail while running in the third spot. Gilbert pulled away on the ensuing restart, but the yellow flag waved again on lap sixteen after Cash's Ford smacked the guardrail (a fate better than the night he sailed out of the park and wound up submerged in the drainage ditch outside turn one). A three-car crash prompted the race's next caution, just before the midway point.

On the restart, Patrick grabbed the second spot from McLaren in turn four and began chasing down the front-running Gilbert. A crash by Ohio driver Fred Dillow brought out the night's final caution and set up a single-file restart, which offered Patrick his best opportunity.

While he got close to Gilbert's rear bumper, Patrick was unable make the pass. With four laps remaining he mounted one last charge but bobbled trying to pressure Gilbert. He watched the gold Chevelle pull away, ending any chance of collecting the bounty.

Gilbert led the parade to the checkers as Patrick finished second, followed by Adkins, McLaren, Dan Aldridge, Swartz, Buddy Medlock, Steve Edmisten, and Snowden.

Floyd Gilbert's autograph from the 1972 season. (Author's collection)

Fans gathered as Gilbert posed for the obligatory victory photograph next to the flag stand, a broad smile atop his beard as he clutched the checkered flag. Despite displaying the creases, dents, and jagged edges from five months of close-quarters beating and banging, the Chevelle's gold metalflake paint still glistened beneath the mercury vapor lights.

The night's sweep marked the third time Gilbert had turned the hat trick of qualifying fastest and winning every race he entered. He came back a week later and rang up another sweep en route to scoring his tenth feature win against another group of worthy challengers.

With season victory No. 33 in the books and photos taken, Gilbert drove back into the shadowed pit area, where the machine was idled up onto the trailer. Someone reached into a cooler and handed Gilbert a cold beer, which he thoughtfully wrapped with his faded red shop rag—in a dry county where alcohol was illegal—and took a long, satisfying swig.

Some weeks you eat steak.

CHAPTER 2:

Paying His Dues

Floyd Wallace Gilbert entered this world on December 23, 1929, in Cincinnati, Ohio, just as the Great Depression was tightening its grip on American families. Growing up during the Depression and the decade of world conflict that followed made people independent, resilient, and strong.

"We was raised in California, Ohio there by the golf course, there by the hill," Gilbert recalled to DirtFans.com. "We would go up there at nighttime with a wash bucket and get in the reservoir and feel with our feet. And sometimes we would come out with one- to two-hundred and maybe even three-hundred golf balls. The reservoir was right in line with the tee and they would probably drop a dozen of them in the water every day. We would get them with our feet, we would get ten cents apiece for them. We got a bucket full one night and some guy took them and sold them, and I never seen him since.

"It was a great time living out in California, Ohio. It was a great place to be raised," Floyd said.

California was a tiny Ohio River community just southeast of Cincinnati, near the Coney Island Amusement Park. It was a short drive from Glen Este Speedway, also once known as Cincinnati Speed Bowl. In the fall of 1951—the track's initial year of operation—Floyd Gilbert experienced his first taste of competition in a demolition derby.

7

"Charlie, our landlord, said they got a race at Glen Este Speedway. He said they got a demolition. He said, 'I got a 1937 Plymouth here, we ought to take it up and try to win it.' Couple hundred dollars to win. So, the demolition derby would have been the first thing I got into, in the fall, second to last race of the year," Gilbert told DirtFans.com. "Generally, in demo, there isn't anything left. I even got rolled. I think I would have won it if I hadn't got it rolled. We took it home and beat it out, put some roll bars in it, and raced it the next Sunday in a regular race. And we did real well; if we hadn't lost a wheel... Anyway, the car wasn't really fast. It had a six cylinder, and off come the right rear wheel leading the consy, and that was the end of the day and the year."

Floyd's career began driving a Plymouth in a 1951 demolition derby at Ohio's former Glen Este Speedway. They returned the following week to compete in the stock car races. (Courtesy DirtFans.com)

But Gilbert was hooked; he returned to the track behind the wheel of a Hudson Terraplane, a car favored by Depression-era gangsters John Dillinger and Baby Face Nelson for its speed and durability.

"Terraplane looked like a 1948 Plymouth. They had unusually strong motors. We never had to do nothing but knock the fenders off and put in some make-believe roll bars and a seat belt, and it made a pretty good race car," Floyd recalled. "The only thing bad about them is they had dippers for oiling: rod dippers. I stayed with Hudson twelve years. Hudson came out with the Big Six in nineteen forty-eight. You could only use an engine that was no newer than ten years. I spent two or three days grinding the serial number off the block. We put that motor in and started making a few bucks. Matter of fact, I got a trophy back then from Lawrenceburg Speedway: third place driver of the year."

Despite a lengthy career filled with famous cars, Gilbert counted the Hudson, which wore the number 6 1/2, as his favorite.

"You could turn it sideways and wasn't nothing getting by. And the engines were very powerful for a flathead six. You could take a two hundred thirty-two cubic inch head and put it on a three oh eight and the twin H power, which was two single-throat carbs, and you got a race engine for a hundred dollars. Hell, they would run with flathead V-eights. The old Hudson handled great; you didn't have to do hardly anything to them. They were way ahead of their time," he told Dirt-Fans.com.

For a time, before he had a tow vehicle, Gilbert would leave the Hudson parked at Glen Este, drive out on Sunday, transfer the battery from his street car, race, then pull the battery out and drive home—usually with winner's money in his pocket.

9

Gilbert's first real success came behind the wheel of a series of Studebakers. Here Floyd drives No. 6½ at the Glen Este Speedway in 1954. (Courtesy DirtFans.com)

Floyd had his share of crashes and wound up in the hospital a couple of times, but likely his worst wreck occurred at Indiana's Lawrenceburg Speedway in the early 1950s.

"I had a good reputation; I could take and drive anything. So, come feature time, the old car I towed down there broke. We used to tow them with a chain. So, this guy with an old thirty-seven Plymouth said, 'Here, Floyd, take mine.' And later on, he furnished me figure-eight cars, but I had to start on the tail and guarantee I'm gonna get me some of this money. We went in the number one turn and they didn't have the wheels plated, and the right rear wheel come off. It dug in the ground, I did a barrel roll, seat belt broke, and I did not turn loose of that steering wheel. I had a death grip on it. Fact is, damn good thing I did. So, I ended up upside down; I had to let myself down out of it. It pulled my shoulder out of place."

Headlines like "Gilbert Wins" and "Gilbert Wins Again" appeared with more frequency in area newspapers during the second half of the 1950s. He became one of the dominant drivers at Glen Este, racing with and regularly beating Bernie and Ralph Latham and Carl Kiser.

The Lathams, Kiser, and some others were lured to another track in 1956. The Cincinnati Race Bowl was a paved 3/8-mile oval featuring late-model stock cars of the Championship Stock Car Circuit. The track became a playground for Kentuckian Nelson Stacy, who went on to win multiple championships in the Midwest Auto Racing Circuit (forerunner of ARCA) and later became a star in NASCAR. The Race Bowl featured the new MARC cars on a weekly basis, and quickly became a battleground between Stacy and Michigan's Iggy Katona.

Floyd, however, stayed with dirt. A 1958 story in the *Cincinnati Enquirer* asked, "Who can beat Floyd Gilbert and his 1954 Hudson is the question at Glen Este, since he's won most of the races?"

Later that same season, Gilbert's car was damaged in a preliminary race when the machine of Mel Brock slammed the guardrail, bounced high into the air, and landed on Gilbert's hood. That same night, Jay Wyatt ran over another car's gas tank and needed first aid after his car was engulfed in flames.

Gilbert made headlines of a different kind in July 1959 when he was among a group of people who tried to rescue a 6-year-old boy, who was apparently exploring a construction site when the ground gave way beneath his feet and he was trapped by the cave-in. Floyd told authorities he had been operating a crane at the site and warned the boy to stay away from the area, but he came back and fell in. A couple dozen volunteers unsuccessfully tried to rescue the child, who later died.

Back on the race track, Gilbert narrowly lost the 1960 Glen Este championship to Ralph Latham, but claimed the 1961 Glen Este season title, despite a couple of vicious crashes.

Floyd's car was "demolished in a spectacular crash" after slamming into Glen Este's outer retaining wall in May 1961, according to one account. Just a month later, his car "smashed through" the retaining wall, according to another. Amazingly, Gilbert was back behind the wheel and picked up a victory the following Saturday at Lawrenceburg, Indiana.

On July 7, 1961, Gilbert won both Glen Este preliminary races and the thirty-lap feature—the first driver to ever sweep at Glen Este, according to the *Cincinnati Enquirer*.

Gilbert's name also regularly appeared in stories promoting upcoming races, along with Ralph Latham and Chuck McWilliams.

That season's wildest outcome unfolded at Glen Este in early August, as race winner Chuck McWilliams finished the event upside down, climbed out, and chased Gilbert on foot.

"[McWilliams] leaped from his inverted chariot and started across the infield, brandishing an iron pipe. Apparently, he was seeking Floyd Gilbert, driver of the car that he thought had caused the flip," according to a story in the *Cincinnati Enquirer*, which claimed a "riot" ensued. The race was called, with McWilliams credited as the winner; Gilbert finished second. "When last seen, McWilliams and Gilbert were shaking hands," according to the newspaper.

Later that season, Floyd was crowned the 1961 Glen Este champion, withstanding the challenges of McWilliams, Jay Wyatt, and Boots Peterson.

The wins came even more frequently in the 1960s. In May 1963, Floyd won a ten-lap heat race, finished second in the 25-lap feature behind veteran John Hill in the Flying ZERO, and won a five-lap backup race: drivers circling the track in reverse. News accounts from the era also show Floyd winning regularly in both figure-eight racing and Classic Stocks at Northern Kentucky Race Bowl, forerunner of Northern Kentucky Speedway and Lawrenceburg Speedway in Indiana. In August 1963, Floyd won the heat race and the 25-lap stock car feature, as well as finishing second to Chuck McWilliams in the figure-eight race at Northern.

Floyd also tried driving modified sprint cars at Lawrenceburg Speedway during that era, with some spectacular results. He finished in a dead heat for second-place in 1962 and, in May 1963, he was one of two drivers to flip their cars during the feature. Floyd just left his car upside down in the infield until the race was completed, according to one news account.

As the 1960s wore on, Gilbert was a regular contender for victory at Northern Kentucky, Glen Este, Lawrenceburg and other tracks, competing against the likes of Ralph Latham, Chuck McWilliams, Billy Teegarden (who abandoned the modifieds for stock cars) George Bauer, Gene Crittenden, Gene Cleveland, Paul Crockett, Pat Patrick, Jay Wyatt, Baldy McLaren, Joe Burdette, Joe Pflum, Ross Smith, and Boots Peterson.

Auto racing was so popular in the Tri-State area promoters staged winter races inside the Cincinnati Gardens, where Gilbert, Ralph Latham, Pat Patrick, sprint car star Dick Gaines, Earl Smith and Kentucky racer Tony Schiller were among the winners.

During the winter months in the 1960s, racers would compete indoors at the Cincinnati Gardens. Here Floyd is pictured with car owner Bob Blair after winning in Blair's Renault. (Courtesy DirtFans.com)

In August 1964, Floyd won a Northern Kentucky stock car feature and the figure-eight feature on the same night.

"Back in the early sixties, I never really ran good. I really struggled; a hundred dollars on the weekend, and you thought you was rich on Monday. But you paid your gas bill. That's the first thing you would do, because you damn sure knew you were going to need some more Friday. I worked up a good credit. I guess I raced on credit," Floyd told DirtFans.com.

Gilbert also won races driving a No. 3 Chevrolet for body shop owner Tommy Simmons.

"No one could beat Ralph Latham or his brother Bernie," Gilbert told *Stock Car Racing* magazine in a 1975 interview. But Floyd beat them or ran with them consistently. Latham won Northern's 1965 championship race, with Gene Crittenden second and Gilbert a close third.

Floyd enjoyed some real success driving for car owner Bob Busener in a string of No. 9 and No. 195 Chevrolets. They raced primarily on the tight Glen Este dirt quarter-mile, the 3/8-mile Northern Kentucky Speedway in nearby Florence, Kentucky, and the quarter-mile dirt track at Lawrenceburg, Indiana.

The team had some help in the pits in 1965 in the form of fifteen-year-old Rodney Combs, a Kentucky native infatuated with auto racing and eager to learn as much as he could. He quickly grew to appreciate Busener and Floyd, whom he first befriended during his Hudson days.

"Floyd picked me up, and I just wanted to learn everything. My pay was bologna sandwiches and beans and wieners—that's

In this 1964 image, Floyd celebrates a victory in the Bob Busener No. 195 1957 Chevrolet. Gilbert credited Busener with getting him out of the "junkers." The credits on the fender include a young Rodney Combs who was a teenager at the time. (Courtesy DirtFans.com)

what Floyd ate—and you got into the race track. That was his first real break driving a strong dirt late model. That car had muffler pipe for roll cage, and it was covered up with roll insulation. I learned a lot mechanically, working on engines, transmissions, rear ends..." said Combs, who would go on to forge his own Dirt Hall of Fame career and compete in NASCAR's premier series for several seasons.

"Bob, that guy was unbelievable. That guy was a mastermind. He was a sharp individual and a neat guy to be around," Combs said in a 2018 interview. "Floyd got the Busener one ninety-five deal, and that was his first true good person he really drove for in late models. That was 1965; I was helping him [Floyd] and helping Bob."

Combs recalled Gilbert had a unique way of measuring time and distance.

"His big thing wasn't how far it was to a race track. It wasn't an hour, or how far, but how many beers it took to get there, whether it was one beer, three beers, six beers," Combs said. "Back then, they all had their little drinking; I guess some guys called it false courage, but he was the same if he drank one or six. It didn't change Floyd. He could do the same whether he had one or three or six. Some of them had to do it to stand on the gas, I guess."

Sometimes Mother Nature called at the most inopportune times.

"One night at Florence, the feature was under caution and Floyd stopped Busener's car at the top of turn three, jumped out, and ran up and over the banking," Combs said. "That place used to have no wall, no guardrail, and he stopped up on the bank, gets out, and takes off. We start to go that way, but then he comes back and gets back in the car. He had to pee, so he just ran over the bank."

Dabbling in ARCA

Buoyed by the successes of 1965, Gilbert and Busener made a major step up for 1966 and entered a series of Automobile Racing Club of America new car series races. ARCA was a major touring series viewed as a Midwestern rival to NASCAR.

Floyd made his first appearance in Florida on Daytona International Speedway's massive 2.5-mile track for the 1966 ARCA 100, driving a No. 9 Ford Galaxie owned by Bob Blair. Simmons Body Shop adorned the rear fender: a deal in exchange for sanding off the second-hand car's old number and painting on a new No. 9, Kevin Blair recalls. On February 13, 1966, Gilbert started and finished fifth out of ten cars in a ten-lap ARCA qualifying race, that was similar but shorter than NASCAR's twin 125s contested later in Speed Weeks. That finish earned Floyd a 13th-place starting spot in the following weekend's 100-lap ARCA season opener.

Floyd Gilbert poses next to the No. 9 1964 Ford Galaxie he raced in the 1966 ARCA 200 at Florida's Daytona International Speedway. The car was owned by Bob Blair and represented Floyd's lone superspeedway appearance. (Courtesy Eddie Roche, Florida Motorsports Retrospective)

A pre-race newspaper wire story listed a dozen names—including Gilbert—as pre-race favorites, despite his lack of superspeedway experience. But Floyd completed just two laps, and is credited with a 29th-place finish. Ohioan Jack Bowsher collected the victory, and dirt rival Ralph Latham finished sixth.

Others in the field included United States Auto Club star and former NASCAR driver Sal Tovella, perennial ARCA title contender and former Daytona winner Iggy Katona, and future ARCA and NASCAR champion Benny Parsons.

"If you don't have the equipment, don't waste your time at Daytona," Gilbert told *Stock Car Racing's* Carroll Hamilton in 1975. He offered a different insight to longtime friend, crew member, and race official Mike Roland decades later. "Everything was fine until the air picked up my car and put it in another lane!"

The official results also show Gilbert was paid $500 for his 29th-place finish, the same amount paid to every driver who finished from seventh through last place.

Back home in the Midwest, feature wins, heat race victories, and headlines came more frequently in 1966, as Floyd spent more time racing stockers while still dabbling with figure-eight and demolition derbies. Once the tracks closed, Gilbert, Chuck McWilliams and other stars continued to race indoors at the Cincinnati Gardens.

Bob Busener's No. 9 Chevelle, with a black vinyl top and big block Chevy engine, was driven by Floyd Gilbert at several ARCA races on both dirt and asphalt in 1966 and 1967. This was taken at the old Dayton, Ohio Speedway. (Steve Struve photo)

Floyd's infatuation with vinyl top Chevelles seemingly began in 1966, with the white No. 9 1966 Chevelle prepared by Busener that had an engine by Jim Stall. The car was sponsored by Ruth Motors in Glencoe, Kentucky, a group that would eventually field its own hugely successful cars and recruit Floyd to drive. He made regular visits to victory lanes at Tri-State tracks around his Cincinnati base while making at least three other ARCA starts

He won a heat race and ran third at Northern Kentucky on June 4. On August 7, Floyd earned his second win at Northern Kentucky. His third came on September 11, after outrunning fast qualifier Jay Wyatt.

In April 1967, he wheeled Busener's Chevelle to a fourth-place finish in the 100-lap ARCA show at Northern Kentucky Speedway, despite blowing the engine with four laps remaining. He raced on the paved Toledo, Ohio Speedway later that month, and posted an eighth-place finish as Iggy Katona took the win in his Dodge. In mid-May, Floyd ran the one of the longest races of his career at the Nashville Fairgrounds Speedway, after being rained out twice the previous weekend. Starting seventeenth on the paved, high-banked half-mile, they ran the entire 300-lap distance on Saturday night; Andy Hampton was the winner.

ARCA records are incomplete from that era, but Floyd's name appeared on the entry lists of at least three other series races, including the inaugural Red Bud 500, a 500-lap torture test on Anderson, Indiana's paved quarter-mile Sun Valley Speedway, in a No. 90 1967 Chevelle; the Dayton 500 at Dayton, Ohio's banked half-mile oval; and a 100-lap race that October at the Louisville Downs horse track.

During that time, a young mechanic named Morgan Chandler did some work for them and helped the team. Their paths would cross again later.

Despite his traveling, Floyd finished fourth in Glen Este's final 1967 late model standings. Pat Patrick won the track points championship, followed by Gene Crittenden, Don Lamb, Gilbert and Baldy McLaren. Bruce Gould finished in eighth place and Joe Burdette tenth.

Gilbert also remained a regular at Northern Kentucky Speedway, winning a half-dozen feature races but narrowly losing the points title.

Gilbert outran Billy Teegarden, Gene Crittenden, and George Bauer September 9 to move from fourth to third in points but could get no closer. Bauer won the season championship race, while Teegarden took the points title.

Tri-County Speedway Opens in 1968

Cincinnati's dirt track racing landscape changed dramatically in 1968 when promoter Bill Redwine opened Tri-County Speedway, a lightning fast half-mile dirt oval with amenities well ahead of its time, in West Chester, Ohio.

Not surprisingly, Floyd was among the track's earliest winners. He posted the fastest time during an open practice session the week before Tri-County's first race. On opening day, April 7, Floyd set fast time of 25.07 seconds, then won the fast dash and a heat race. After leading early, his No. 7 1967 Chevelle suffered a broken axle—but Floyd still finished fifth. He collected $675 for his feature and fast heat race wins the following week in the Chevelle, which was owned by Don Campbell and Jake Brusman, according to a *Cincinnati Enquirer* story penned by Bill Brodrick; the same Bill Brodrick who later became the famed Union 76 "hat man" in NASCAR victory lanes.

Floyd became Tri-County's first two-time winner May 4, taking the feature by six car-lengths over Chuck McWilliams and Bruce Gould.

"Tri-County was kind of the Daytona of race tracks. That place was way ahead of its time," Rodney Combs said in a 2018 interview.

Floyd was a force at Tri-County, often dominating preliminaries and features. He won a 25-lap feature May 25, holding off rivals McWilliams and Baldy McLaren. He repeated that performance June 1, besting McWilliams and Bruce Gould. By June 11, Floyd had earned his fifth Tri-County feature victory of the young season, wheeling the Chevelle through an early duel with Ross Smith, then holding off John Mugavin and Smith for the checkers. Gilbert advanced into the feature by finishing second to Joey Stricker in the consolation race.

John Campbell, nephew of Don Campbell, recounted a spat between

Floyd and Tri-County promoter Bill Redwine.

"I remember pretty vividly that Bill Redwine, owner of Tri-County had warned Floyd over his t-shirt and jeans while driving. He insisted all drivers wear professional suits," Campbell recalled. "Floyd apparently didn't go along with that, and Redwine confronted him in the pits and fined him five dollars. They were both standing at the pit entrance on the backstretch near turn two. Floyd whipped out a twenty-dollar bill, slapping it in Redwine's hand saying, 'There's your five dollars and some more, go buy yourself a steak.' With that he loaded up and left the track."

After starting 1968 driving Jim Stall's No. 7 Chevelle, Gilbert reunited with Bob Busener to drive his No. 195 Chevelle. Here Floyd and crew members work on the car at the Tri-County Speedway. (Courtesy Greg Courtney)

Racing on Wednesday and Saturday nights, Tri-County regularly attracted USAC stock car champion Butch Hartman, pavement star Don Gregory, and other top names from across the Midwest, to mix it up with all the Cincinnati-area regulars.

Gilbert amassed four early feature wins and held the Tri-County points lead through the first part of the season, but he lost the top spot to Chuck McWilliams on June 26. Floyd missed that night as McWilliams reset the track record and won his second straight, with John Mugavin second and Dick Dunlevy third.

Gilbert won often at Tri-County, but the competition and costs continued mounting. He even drove a Dodge Charger a couple of times, finishing third behind Jay Wyatt's Flying ZERO and Chuck McWilliams on July 7 before returning to a Chevelle. He finished a car-length behind those same two Mopars driven by Wyatt and McWilliams on July 20.

As summer wore on Floyd, Campbell, and Brusman parted ways. Floyd reunited with Bob Busener and his No. 195 1967 Chevelle as Don Lamb slid behind the wheel of the No. 7.

"Floyd used to say Tri-County was 'too nice,'" Larry Moore stated in a 2017 interview, "because it had a driver's shower with hot water in the pits."

Gilbert returned to the Tri-County winner's circle August 10, just a week after Don White upset A.J. Foyt to win a USAC stock car race there. Floyd steered Busener's Chevelle past Chuck McWilliams by inches. On August 14, Floyd won again by besting Gene Petro and fast qualifier Pat Patrick.

The victories pushed Gilbert back into second place in the Tri-County standings, but he lost that spot August 21 as Pat Patrick celebrated his 28th birthday with a Wednesday night victory over Billy Teegarden.

Floyd continued to slide, finishing fifth on August 28, behind Pat Patrick, Hartman, McWilliams and Don Lamb. Three nights later, mechanical problems forced him to the pits while leading the feature as McWilliams captured his fifteenth victory of the year. Floyd finished third behind Tommy Simmons and Lennie Waldo on September 20.

On September 28, Gilbert reset Jay Wyatt's Tri-County qualifying record—seemingly the exclusive property of the Hemi Dodge drivers—to 22.02 seconds. He finished third in that night's feature, however, behind Butch Hartman and Don Gregory.

McWilliams ultimately edged out Pat Patrick to capture Tri-County's first championship with 18 feature wins in 32 starts, driving the Skilcraft Sheet Metal Dodge owned by the Anderson brothers of Hebron, Kentucky.

The car was originally prepared by Harry Hyde, and formerly raced on the NASCAR Grand National circuit by Earl Balmer and Gordon Johncock. McWilliams got acquainted with the car with a fourth-place debut in the car in February's ARCA 200 at Daytona.

Despite winning more than $13,000 in prize money at Tri-County, McWilliams told Brodrick in an *Enquirer* story that the team lost money due to the expense of maintaining the Hemi engines.

At Glen Este's Greater Cincinnati Race Bowl, Floyd held off Pat Patrick to win the 50-lap season championship race in late September, but it wasn't enough; Patrick claimed that track's points championship for the second straight season.

Tragedy Ushers in 1969

High expectations surrounded the start of the 1969 season, but the year began tragically. On opening day the 38-year-old Busener suffered a fatal heart attack working on the team's Chevelle in the Tri-County pits. Gilbert ultimately purchased the race cars from Busener's widow and raced on.

Tri-County again ran its weekly shows on Wednesday and Saturday nights. Early on, Floyd finished second to Billy Teegarden in a 25-lap feature April 30, came in fourth on May 14, led laps late in the going before ultimately finishing third behind Teegarden and Don Lamb in a 50-lap feature May 30, and then ran third in a June 4 Wednesday night show behind Bruce Gould and Ralph Latham.

Floyd went to Tri-County's victory lane June 14 after early leaders Carl Kiser and Joe Burdette got together in turn one on a rain-slickened race track. The crash sent Burdette's Chevelle over the rail to land on its top, bringing out the red flag. The race was restarted but flagged at lap thirty of fifty due to the speedway's curfew. Fast qualifier Billy Teegarden finished second.

By mid-July, Floyd was in back in fifth place in the Tri-County standings, trailing eight-race winner McWilliams, Teegarden, Gould, and Gene Cleveland. He finished third behind rising ARCA star Ramo Stott and Larry Moore on July 26, after watching McWilliams and Teegarden crash on the final lap.

At Glen Este, Floyd narrowly lost to Vern LeFevers June 8. Floyd's first

Glen Este victory of the season occurred on July 13, as he wheeled the Chevelle past Rodney Combs. He later ran second to Ralph Latham in Jim Cook's ZERO Plymouth at Tri-County on August 16.

During that time, Floyd began turning his attention away from just Tri-County and Glen Este, competing at other area other tracks, winning at Springfield, Ohio and Clay City, Kentucky, and running well at Eldora Speedway in Rossburg, Ohio.

He finished second behind Larry Moore and just ahead of fast qualifier Dick DeBolt at Eldora on August 24. Floyd won the 50-lap season championship race at Glen Este on September 21, but narrowly lost the points title to John Mugavin, who claimed seven feature victories. Gilbert was the fastest qualifier but spun twice early in the race, forcing him to roar through the pack. He passed Baldy McLaren on the 20th lap and led to the checkers while Mugavin finished second in his GTO.

Floyd finished fifth in the final Tri-County standings while Chuck Mc-Williams won his second straight title driving a newer Hyde-prepared Hemi Dodge. Billy Teegarden finished second.

On September 27, Floyd raced to a third-place at Tri-County behind Pat Patrick and Joey Stricker on Saturday night, then went to Clay City on Sunday. There, he set fast time, won the fast car dash, and finished second in the 30-lap feature to local standout J.C. Stone. Gilbert had grown quite fond of Clay City, winning regularly in its NASCAR-sanctioned program racing against Stone, his brother Carl Stone, Armon Smith, and other talented locals plus Cincinnatian Joe Burdette.

Floyd finished third in Tri-County's October 18 feature after Pat Patrick bumped Billy Teegarden while battling for second on the final turn of the final lap. Both spun, allowing Gene Cleveland and Gilbert to slip by. Teegarden slammed his Dodge into reverse and crossed the start-finish line backwards to finish fourth, taking a slim four-point lead in the season standings over Chuck McWilliams. Floyd wasn't a factor in the 100-lap season championship race, which was dominated by McWilliams. Larry Moore and Pat Patrick finished second and third, while Teegarden wound up tenth after suffering a flat tire.

CHAPTER 3:

Floyd's Kentucky Home

R ival John Mugavin once told Gilbert he was a "legend in his own time in Kentucky." Who was Floyd to argue?

Many of the major victories in his Hall of Fame career and his two most significant winning streaks occurred primarily on Kentucky ovals. Most of his career highlights came while driving for Kentucky car owners Lloyd Ruth, Morgan Chandler, and R.L. Duncan.

No easy pickings, Kentucky boasted some superb homegrown driving talent and nowhere was Floyd more successful than Clay City Raceway, a half-mile oval in a rural farming community two hours south of his Cincinnati home.

Mention his name to the old-timers, the ones looking on from greying wooden bleachers and watch a wry smile creep across their faces as a gleam rises in their eyes like the sun coming up. Listen as they lapse into stories of threading the needle by splitting two slower cars entering turn three at Clay City, hitting the wall at Ponderosa and still coming home the victor, running the high lane at Florence, or running away from the field at Bluestone on muggy summer nights.

Gilbert raced all over central Kentucky and usually found success. Not surprisingly, Floyd told DirtFans.com most of his favorite tracks were in the Bluegrass state.

"I like Glen Este [Ohio]. I liked Northern Kentucky, Clay City, More-head, Richmond, especially when I drove for Duncan. That car really handled well there. I liked the 'little Daytona' in Danville. I always called it Danville because I could never think of the name of the track [Pon-derosa Speedway]... I liked Whitewater Valley Speedway in Indiana, too. It was a tight little track. Take a breath and you were in the next turn," Floyd said. "Mainly my favorite tracks were in Kentucky. The people treated me well.

Call it superstition, routine, or habit, but Floyd was almost always the first racer at Clay City's pit gate on Friday or Sunday afternoons.

Flyin' Floyd Gilbert relaxes with the checkered flag after capturing one of about 500 feature race wins, many which occurred at tracks across Kentucky. (Photo by SMP, cour-tesy Fremont Speedway Hall of Fame and Mid-American Auto Racing News archives)

"Well, generally I had kind of a set thing that I did. I would leave at noon, even to Clay City, and in two or three hours I would be down there, just taking my time. Very calm, very relaxed. Many times—well, not many times, but at least two that I forgot to get me a beer and it was on the other side of the bus. So, I would set the old bus aimed dead straight, and I would get up and get me a beer and get back before I crashed. Another time, you know the turn-off of I-75 onto I-64 going east? It's kind of a tight turn. I made that twice doing seventy miles an hour with that bus, hauling that race car," he told DirtFans.com.

Floyd first ventured to Clay City in 1968, running some races in the track's NASCAR points program and finishing 20th in the Modified standings. He made Clay City a more regular stop in 1969, when the NASCAR feature class was late model stock, and Gilbert just missed making the track's top ten.

All those wins made a big impression. Fan Shirley Briscoe recalls the time Floyd parked his school bus/racecar hauler at a local service station, just off the Mountain Parkway. "A young boy didn't notice who Floyd was," she said. "He said to Floyd, 'no point in you going to race here.' Floyd replied, 'Why's that?' The boy replied, 'Because Floyd Gilbert will blow the doors off your car.' Floyd couldn't stop laughing."

Former racer, crewman and journalist Tom Lesshaft fondly recalls those times.

"Some of my favorite memories were getting to Clay City early on Friday afternoons and sitting in Floyd's bus, 'Beulah,' and listening to him tell stories," Lesshaft said in a 2018 interview. "Floyd would sit in there and drink a couple beers, and he was just fearless. And he was fast."

The Chevelle that normally rode on that old school bus was sometimes Gilbert's backup car when he was driving for other people. If his primary ride wasn't available or had problems, Floyd had something to race.

"A lot of times I could fall on the tail of the feature and still make money. It was insurance," Gilbert said.

One night at another track, other drivers refused to race against him. "It happened down in Kentucky, when I drove for old man Clary out of Louisville. They had a driver's meeting and said, 'we don't want to let him run.' So, guess what happened? It rained and I laughed all the way home. First I laughed at them, then I laughed all the way home."

Another time, things weren't so funny.

Running a big race at the old Somerset Sportsdrome in southeast

Kentucky, Floyd and car owner John Holmes were convinced they had earned the victory, but track officials said they'd scored Gilbert a lap down and local favorite Glen Bolin of Danville was the winner. Bolin was a double amputee at age 13, losing both his left arm and leg, but a successful racer in his No. 1 Chevrolet.

"Floyd went down there in John Holmes' car, and he lapped Bolin and all of them. He went to get paid and they said, 'You weren't the winner, you were a lap down.' Floyd was fighting mad, but they gave it to Bolin," J.T. LeFever recalled decades later. But that wasn't the end of the story. "John Holmes had some property down in Kentucky, down in that same area. He went down there to mow and thought it would be funny, so he wrote this letter to Floyd—as if it was from Bolin—said it was an honor to beat such a great legend. So, he mailed it. Well when Floyd got it, he got so mad John was afraid to tell him.

"When Floyd came up for his Hall of Fame induction, he met me at Valley Radiator and we camped at Florence that week," LeFever continued. "We were sitting there one night and John Holmes said, 'Floyd, I'm going to tell you a story, but I don't want you to get mad at me.' Floyd said, 'I'm not gonna get mad.' And John told that story, that he was the one who sent the letter. Floyd just laughed."

Gilbert's later success was so linked to the Bluegrass state that several newspapers, magazines and track promoters mistakenly listed him as being from a variety of Kentucky towns, including Covington, Independence, Dry Ridge, and Glencoe.

Fittingly, the National Dirt Late Model Hall of Fame that enshrined him is in Florence, just behind a race track where he found great success.

CHAPTER 4:

Rough & Tumble

Through the first two decades of his driving career, Floyd Gilbert's burning desire to win races sometimes created collateral damage along the way. It was an era when short track success was often determined by the steel of a man's nerve and his front bumper. Carroll Hamilton addressed it well in his 1975 profile in *Stock Car Racing* magazine, where he rebranded him "Fightin' Floyd Gilbert, Inc."

"These were the years when the roughest and toughest won, when putting a guy into the wall was just part of the game and Floyd was good at the game," Hamilton wrote. "His reputation as a 'rough' and 'dirty' driver was formed in these early years, and despite his later-gained finesse and smooth driving style, the reputation has stuck."

Many of Floyd's former rivals remember his penchant for winning, whatever it took.

"I've run with a lot of unique characters in the series I've run: Larry Phillips, [Scott] Bloomquist, [Jeff] Purvis, Floyd Gilbert, and Billy Teegarden. But I've got to say, out of all of them, Floyd Gilbert was probably the most unique individual I've ever been around," fellow Dirt Hall of Fame driver Larry Moore recalled in 2017. "Gilbert would spin people out and rarely hurt himself. He was really good at it."

Asked who was the toughest driver he competed against in his forty-plus-year career, Kentucky standout E.M. Snowden Jr., listed a dozen— but "Floyd Gilbert" was the first name out of his mouth.

"Floyd and Billy Teegarden, they were really tough. For a while there, they were running with Pappy Clary out of Louisville," Snowden said. "That was a roughneck bunch. They would put the bumper to you, if they could catch you."

Rodney Combs offered a much different impression.

"He was tough. He didn't tear up stuff, and he took care of his equipment. He knew if he finished, he would make money—and he had his own stuff, and if you tear it up you don't make money because you've got to fix it," Combs said. "He drove straight, and I learned that from him. Chuck McWilliams did, too. The other ones were all crooked and sideways. The straighter you run, the faster you run. I always said you had to have courage to drive it down there straight into the corner instead of throwing it sideways, because then you turned your back to that wall. He was smart, and he was good when it came to the slick tracks."

Driving the partially obscured the No. 195 Chevelle, Gilbert works his way through traffic at Ohio's Glen Este Speedway in 1969. Ahead of him are Robin Hayes (43), Mike Combs (48), and Rodney Combs (47). (Courtesy DirtFans.com)

Even when Gilbert drove for others, he usually hauled a car everywhere with his old modified school bus—either as a backup if his primary had trouble, or he would put someone else in his car. One night at Whitewater Valley Speedway in Indiana, Floyd was driving Clary's GTO, so he invited Larry Moore to race the backup car.

In a 2017 interview, Moore recounted how he started to sneak into the pits without paying but Gilbert made him go back and purchase a pit pass, "because it was unlucky." Later, Moore was looking inside the car's cockpit and pulled a billy club from beneath the seat.

"Put that back in there," Floyd said. "Why? Why do I need a billy club?" Moore asked. "'Because this car don't handle too well and the brakes aren't too good, so you may need it after the race.' But he didn't laugh. He was serious," Moore said.

While both finished well, Floyd wasn't satisfied with the outcome.

"When I drove his car, he was running third and I was running fifth, but we both put the wrong tires on. Well, the guy who was leading came off turn four and blew a radiator hose. Floyd went from third to first, and I went from fifth to third. After the race, he bitched at me. 'Why didn't you run second?' I said, 'If the guy hadn't blew the radiator hose, you would have run third.' He said, 'Well, I knew he was going to; didn't you see that thing steaming?'"

Moore thought enough of those and other Gilbert stories to include them in his own biography, *On Top of the World*.

Gilbert's style got smoother as the quality of his rides improved, but he still had a habit of brushing slower cars on his way to the front, Moore said.

"He could be hard on lapped cars and spin them when he didn't have to," Moore said. "I did the same thing; Dale Earnhardt was the same way. Donnie Seaborn asked me one time why'd I have to take the paint off them cars when I passed them. He said, 'Try to miss them by three feet instead of three inches.' Floyd would take the paint off the cars when he'd go by them and we had to dodge them, but he rarely ever got caught up in one."

It was the one and only time the future Hall of Famer drove for Gilbert. However, a few weeks later Billy Teegarden wheeled Gilbert's car in another race at Whitewater; the outcome was a bit different.

"Billy T was driving Floyd's car and Floyd was running second, and Floyd put him in the fence," Moore recounted. "After the race, Billy was hot. He told Floyd, 'You MF'er, we were gonna run first and second.' Floyd said, 'Yeah, but the wrong guy was leading.' Billy said, 'You'd wreck your own car to win?' Floyd said, 'Well, I just did.'"

Teegarden used to joke that Gilbert would spin other cars coming through the pack to give his competitors something to dodge.

One night, a situation with Vern LeFevers nearly went too far.

"Floyd and my dad had a problem one time at Whitewater Valley Speedway. Dad had a big lead and broke, so he put his arm out the window going into turn one [to let others know he was slowing down]. Floyd hit him right in the ass and shoved him up into the fence," J.T. LeFever recalled. "Dad proceeded to junk him the next two or three races until the guy who owned Floyd's car—Pappy Clary—asked, 'Are you gonna run here next week?' Dad said, 'Yes.' 'Well, I'll take my car somewhere else, because you've wrecked it three weeks in a row.' Dad said, 'You put him out of it and I won't wreck it.' Floyd got mad and went to get a gun, and my dad met him at his truck and stuck a gun to his nose while he [Gilbert] was reaching for a gun.

"'What are we going to do to end this?' Floyd asked. 'You don't run into me no more, and I won't run into you no more,' LeFevers replied. 'Agreed,' Gilbert said, nodding."

The two rivals let go of their feud and later became good friends. So too did Gilbert and Teegarden, but it was some time after a knock-down, drag-out battle at the bullring in Richmond, Kentucky.

"I was leading with a few [laps] to go and Billy Teegarden hit me. They call it a bump and run. He bumped me and put me in the fluff and ran. So, I caught back up with him on the last lap and I bumped him and I ran," Floyd told DirtFans.com. "He pulled through the infield and waited on me. He wasn't going to let me get to the flag. So, I kind of tricked him. I made him think I was going to the front of him. I had just enough time to cut it and duck behind him and get to the flag. Then there was a big hullabaloo.

"I pulled into his pit and got out. I asked, 'Who wants it first?' Somebody grabbed me from behind and the next thing I know Billy was hitting me. I didn't think that was too kosher because I wanted to knock

31

his head off," Floyd said, laughing. "It was all in the game. The way I felt about racing was if you were going to screw me around, I was going to give it right back to you."

Floyd told DirtFans.com that over time, he learned better ways to race.

"I think when I first started, I was driving greedy, the first ten years or so. A greedy driver is a good driver, if you don't crash out your equipment. And at first, I crashed a lot of race cars—Lawrenceburg, Glen Este, and everywhere. Until finally one day I woke up and said, 'I'm not making any money at this,'" Gilbert said. "So, I started easing up and running halfway back. Not qualifying hard, even starting on the tail. Found out you can win from those positions. They would throw the green flag and I would ease up off the gas and let them go, just sit there and coast for a while. Then start picking them off one at a time. I used that system until the time I quit. Never any hurry. It didn't pay anything until you got to the checkered flag."

In the magazine profile, Hamilton explained that Floyd had no trouble donning the black hat—much like the late Dale Earnhardt—because he recognized that fans loved rivalries.

"If the fans aren't booing or cheering, I'm not doing anything," Gilbert told Hamilton. "Whether they like me or they hate me, they buy a ticket to watch me."

CHAPTER 5:

Turning Pro

Floyd Gilbert's desire to win gave way to his need to win during the 1970 season when at the age of forty, he traded in his union card as a heavy equipment crane operator and made the remarkable career decision to become a professional race car driver—or, in his own words, a "professional bum." Not in NASCAR or ARCA but on the same rough and tumble Midwestern dirt ovals he'd competed on for the previous two decades.

"Racing is a twenty-four-hour-a-day thing with me. I don't think about anything else," Gilbert told the Cincinnati Enquirer in 1970.

Dividing his time between the former Bob Busener No. 195 Chevelle and later that summer, as a hired gun for Ralph "Pappy" Clary's Louisville-based No. 1 GTO, Gilbert piled up wins and captured track championships at the brand-new Whitewater Valley Speedway in Liberty, Indiana, and his first of four in a row at Glen Este Speedway.

The year also marked the emergence of another new rival in the already talent-rich Tri-State region, someone who immediately challenged Gilbert on his home track at Glen Este. At just twenty years old, Rodney Combs was half Gilbert's age, but the youngster—who just a few years before had served as a volunteer crew member for Floyd on the Busener Chevelles, and often rode to the track with Floyd—proved as competitive as his more experienced rival.

Combs won Tri-County Speedway's 1969 hobby stock title, then went to victory lane on the challenging half-mile in only his second late model start, early in the 1970 season. Combs took the lead on the eighth lap and withstood a late charge from fast qualifier Gene Petro. With the 24-car field fully inverted, Petro had to maneuver through traffic, passing Gilbert late in the going, but he was unable to reel in Combs' Chevelle. Gene Cleveland got by Gilbert just before the checkers flew, with Gene Crittenden finishing fifth.

Combs and Gilbert were both shut out the following Sunday at Tri-County as the Hemi Dodges of Gene Cleveland and Chuck McWilliams finished first and second, with Petro third. Floyd won a heat race for the second straight week. Ralph Latham and Pat Patrick were among other spring winners at Tri-County.

Floyd's success driving the No. 195 Chevelles prompted him to begin racing for a living. (Courtesy DirtFans.com)

Glen Este opened in mid-May with Floyd wheeling his '69 Chevelle to fast qualifier honors and the Sunday victory. Combs and his six-cylinder-powered Chevy II won the dash, a heat race, and led early. The following Sunday, Combs took the lead away from fast qualifier Gilbert on lap nineteen of the 25-lap feature and held on for the win, with Pat

Patrick just nipping Floyd for second.

That early success still tastes sweet to Combs.

"I've still got the article; we had a big six-cylinder car and Floyd had a V-Eight. The first race at Glen Este Motor Speedway, and it said 'Teacher beats pupil,' because I ran second to him. The next week it had 'Pupil beats teacher;' I beat him in the second one. I've still got the article, from one of them little papers in Ohio. It was pretty cool, since I helped him all those years and I got to beat him," Combs recalled.

Floyd, however, wasn't so excited.

"He wasn't ready for that. He was proud when I ran second, but he didn't like you beating him. He didn't like to lose," Combs said.

Gilbert retook the Glen Este points lead with a May 30 victory, despite being involved in a crash in a heat race. A couple more wins in June widened his margin before Ron Baker edged him by a nose in the June 28 feature. "With Gilbert running the way he was tonight, I needed everything the car had," Baker told the *Cincinnati Enquirer*.

That spring, some late model drivers got into a dispute with Tri-County promoter Bill Redwine over payout and organized a boycott of the popular half-mile.

With his Saturday nights suddenly free, Floyd traveled to Brownstown, Indiana. Unfortunately, he found the fairgrounds already had its share of hot dogs—including Don Hobbs, Jim Curry, Russ Petro, Ray Godsey, Kenny Simpson, and Ira Bastin—so the pickings were no easier there.

Brownstown was later the scene of the season's longest and likely most unique race, a 250-lap July 4 feature. Late in the going the lights at the track went out for about ten minutes, allowing leader Gene Petro to get out and add five gallons of gas to his fuel cell, according a story in the *Seymour Tribune*. Petro, who was the fastest qualifier, won by eight laps over second-place Dave Moran, but barely had enough fuel to finish. Floyd won the trophy dash but was shut out of the top ten in the feature.

Most Friday nights that summer were spent competing at Whitewater Valley Speedway, which opened as a quarter-mile oval. Floyd assembled four victories in five weeks at Whitewater to take command of the late model points standings. After besting Gene Petro and Baldy McLaren in an August 22 feature, Floyd had more than twice as many points as second place Bob Smith. Others in the top ten included Gerald Dixon, Dick DeBolt, Chick Hale, Gene Petro, Earl Smith, and Larry Moore. Another late season winning streak locked up that track championship.

He enjoyed less success in Kentucky that year, as familiar haunts like Bluestone on Saturdays and Clay City on Sunday afternoons became almost the sole property of J.C. Stone and the Brewer's Chevrolet-backed No. 079 Chevelle. Nicknamed "Mouse," Stone was a farmer with a big right foot who dominated both tracks that season.

Instead, Floyd focused on winning the Glen Este points battle, which was very much in doubt when the track hosted its 100-lap mid-season championship race.

Pat Patrick led the first 50-lap segment before Gilbert passed him on lap 39, but when Chuck McWilliams brought out the caution, the order reverted to the previous completed lap. Gilbert protested in vain. With time running out, Gilbert finished three car-lengths back at the end of the first 50 laps. Patrick and Gilbert got together early in the second segment, with Gilbert spinning and Patrick sent to the rear. Don Lamb inherited the lead, but Floyd passed him with three laps remaining and claimed a $900 victory.

Floyd won four out of five races through August into early September at Glen Este, including a $1,000 payday in the 70-lap Labor Day special—all while driving Clary's car. It was his eighth Glen Este victory of the year, and he went on to easily take that track championship.

Gilbert swept Bluestone October 10, winning the fast dash, fast heat, and feature to finish with 24 feature wins for the season.

It was about that time, Combs said, that Floyd began a new trend: trekking southward in the winter to extend his season.

"In about 1969 or 1970, Floyd was the first one who left the north and went down to Florida and go racing down there. That was in the school bus with fifty-five-gallon drums of gas inside the son-of-a-bitch, with the bologna and the beans and wieners. He'd go down there and kick their butt. He started that. I got to go in 1971, with Jim Stall. He was the dude who started going down there to race in the winter time and make some bucks," Combs recalled, adding he remembers a race at Deland that was so cold people were burning the wooden ramps to their trailers to try and stay warm.

Floyd wheeled the No. 1 Pontiac GTO prepared by Ralph "Pappy" Clary of Louisville, during parts of 1970 and 1971. Here Floyd dices with Gene Petro in the No. 29 Chevelle at Whitewater Valley. (Courtesy DirtFans.com)

CHAPTER 6:

Twenty-one Straight & a Nickname

An off-season game of musical chairs opened the door to a significant opportunity prior to the 1971 season. Ralph Latham left the seat of Morgan Chandler's Queen City Chevrolet-backed Chevelle after a couple of hugely successful seasons and was replaced by Gene Petro. That left Petro's former ride—the vaunted Ruth Motors Chevelle that earned dozens of victories in 1970—in need of a driver.

Floyd took over the powerful white and red Chevelle for owner Lloyd Ruth of Glencoe, Kentucky. Two Holley four-barrel carburetors atop a tunnel ram intake manifold typically jutted through the car's red hood and supplied ample air and fuel to the 470 cubic inch Chevrolet powerplant, making the car as speedy as any. And they certainly proved it during the first three months of the 1971 season.

Most of the tracks awoke from winter slumber in late April or early May, and Gilbert was more than ready. When the gates of Glen Este Speedway opened May 9, Floyd wasted no time shattering the five-year-old track qualifying record of 16.75 seconds, which he'd previously shared with Pat Patrick. His 16.69-second lap gave Gilbert the pole, but he was unable to hold off Ron Baker's Ford for the checkers in the 25-lap feature.

After that night, Floyd and the Ruth Motors Chevelle ripped off an incredible 21 consecutive victories over seven straight weekends at three different tracks. After losing on Mother's Day, Floyd remained unbeaten every weekend until Independence Day.

The incredible string began May 14 at Clay City Raceway's half-mile, which switched to Fridays, continued the following night at Bluestone Speedway in Morehead, Kentucky, and included snaring the first of seven straight victories at Glen Este on Sunday night, May 16. That night he bested runner-up Billy Teegarden in a second Ruth Motors Chevelle, as well as Rodney Combs.

Gilbert later drove the No. 29 Chevelle owned by Kentucky's Lloyd Ruth to 21 consecutive victories in the first half of the 1971 season. Here Gilbert (right) is pictured with Tommy Boots and Art Ruth (center). (Courtesy DirtFans.com)

Reruns were on the menu as spring became summer because Floyd just kept on winning, including a 50-lap race at Glen Este May 30 and holding off teammate Teegarden on June 6 to nab his fourth straight win at Glen Este, and his fourteenth of the young season.

"I was trying to outrun him [Gilbert] and I couldn't," Teegarden told Paul Ritter of the *Cincinnati Enquirer*. "I was handling good the first part of the race, then I had problems; I just couldn't catch him."

Floyd won a 50-lap special race at Clay City June 18. Two nights later, he withstood the challenges of longtime rival Pat Patrick to claim his sixth consecutive Glen Este victory, his twentieth overall feature win in twenty-six starts.

"This time I had to earn it," Floyd told *Enquirer* writer Paul Ritter after the 25-lap feature. Patrick then jokingly told Gilbert, "If I were smart, I would change my car over and race Floyd all the time." Which elicited a typically understated response. "Don't get too smart. I got a good thing going here," Gilbert told Patrick. Pat, in turn, promised to "blow Gilbert's doors off."

Amid the winning streak, the Cincinnati paper did an interview with the seemingly unbeatable Gilbert to try and learn the secrets of his uncanny success. They found he'd mellowed.

"Since I've joined Lloyd Ruth, this is the first year I've really had financial backing, and it has really helped my racing. Having good equipment and spare parts is one of the greatest assets," Floyd admitted.

And what about his reputation as one of the toughest drivers in the business?

"I imagine during my career my temper has hurt me a lot. But I've cooled it down about two hundred percent over the past two years. A lot of people tell me I'm mellowing with age and getting smoother. I can tell it myself. I have to believe it, because I'm winning more races... I'm running better," he said, while admitting he and Pat Patrick had tangled on the track earlier in the year after Patrick tried to spin him.

"For eighteen of the twenty-one years I've been driving, I was like a wild man. I just didn't care. Racing was fun: a chance to drink some beer and have a good time. Then, in 1968, I found I really had an interest in racing. I found out I was as good or better than most of the guys I was running against," Floyd continued. "I drive hard and I drive to win. I don't drive for the glory. I don't drive for the sport. I drive for the money now."

It was the end of June when Floyd equaled Patrick's years old Glen Este record by earning his seventh straight win on the quarter-mile oval. Promoter Fran Rapp offered up a $50 bounty for anyone who beat Gilbert but, once again, nobody could.

"If they were going to give it [bounty] to somebody...if they're going to put it up, then the guy who has to fight hardest to maintain it ought to get it," Floyd told the *Enquirer*. "I was worried tonight. I was more worried about Billy [Teegarden]," he said of his former teammate, who had shown up driving a Hemi-powered Dodge. Billy won a heat race and paced the feature's first six laps before Floyd dove to the bottom, passed him, and led to the checkers. Teegarden ran a strong second, followed by Pat Patrick, Ron Baker, and Vern LeFevers.

Floyd later told DirtFans.com that Teegarden finished second to him a remarkable eighteen times during the streak, which finally ended. Glen Este's Firecracker 50 and a $2,000 purse beckoned the following weekend, but Pat Patrick claimed the prize; Floyd was nowhere to be found, after encountering mechanical problems while racing in Kentucky.

It was about that same time that the season's most dominant combination suddenly, inexplicably split up.

After parting ways with the Ruth Motors team, Floyd drove several machines, including this victorious outing at Whitewater Valley in the No. 1 1957 Chevrolet owned by John Cummins. (Courtesy Fremont Hall of Fame, Mid-American Auto Racing News Archives)

Gilbert then made a few starts in a No. 1 1957 Chevrolet owned by John Cummins. That combination set fast time at Glen Este July 11 and won at Whitewater Valley Speedway the following weekend. Floyd returned to Clay City July 23 and went to victory lane, picking up a $1,000 payday in the Mid-Season Championship race while driving his own No. 11 1965 Chevelle, prepared by son David Gilbert and Doug Marcum. Two nights later, he steered that same car to his 28th feature win of the season and his eighth in eight starts at Glen Este.

Writing in *Mid-American Auto Racing News*, "Cincinnati Scene" columnists Carl and Georgeann Stemler said Gilbert "claims to not be superstitious," but told everyone his big Clay City victory was ordained when the gas pump stopped at 777 for his pre-race fill up.

Somewhere during all that winning is when Floyd gained his nickname of Flyin' Floyd. It began appearing with regularity in columns and race results stories penned by the Stemlers. Where it originated may be lost to history, but the couple receives the credit because their usage is preserved on yellowing pages documenting his remarkable 1971 campaign.

Some of Floyd's Clay City victories came at the expense of Bluegrass State fan favorite Paul "Butterball" Wooldridge, who was also having a monster season. Wooldridge had been winning regularly and leading the points at three Kentucky ovals—Somerset's Lake Cumberland Speedway, Richmond Raceway, and Capitol City Speedway in Frankfort—in the mighty Duncan's Delight Chevelle.

But on Sunday August 1, Wooldridge ventured up to Gilbert's domain at Glen Este, where he qualified second fastest behind Rodney Combs in the Earl's Towing Chevelle. Wooldridge then won both 50-lap segments of Glen Este's Mid-Season Championship in the Duncan Chevelle, He led every lap in the first segment, and needed sixteen circuits to take command of the second segment. Gilbert put on a furious late race charge, but Wooldridge cut him off for the win and left town $1,000 wealthier.

Wooldridge "produced a decisive victory in Gilbert's domain," "delighted the crowd by posting second fast time," and "received a near standing ovation for his victories," Georgeann Stemler wrote in *Mid-American*.

During part of the 1971 season, Floyd successfully fielded his own No. 11 Chevelle, winning often at Clay City and Bluestone speedways in Kentucky and Glen Este, Ohio. (Photo by Steve Cottle, courtesy author's collection)

"We'd heard about this race for about three weeks, and I'd run with most of these boys, so I thought I'd give it a try," Wooldridge told the *Cincinnati Enquirer*. Floyd, however, was less congenial, telling *Mid-American Auto Racing News*, "He has to come up here and run with me in order to beat me. I beat him all the time down in Clay City, and I don't think he can do it here again."

Despite promising to return, Wooldridge failed to show up the following week; Gilbert lapped all but the second-place car of Mike Wilkins. With that August 8 victory, Floyd held a 1,060-point lead over second-place Pat Patrick, and a 2,000-point cushion over third-place Ron Baker.

Floyd roared back the following weekend to establish a Glen Este record by earning his tenth win of the season on August 3.

Others were paying close attention to Gilbert's success at Clay City. The track soon attracted more Cincinnati-area invaders, including Jay Wyatt and George Bauer in ex-Jim Cook ZERO Chargers, and Gene Petro in Morgan Chandler's Chevelle.

Floyd also won some races that summer in Ralph Clary's GTO, but a new door was about to open.

Over in the Chandler camp, veteran Gene Petro did an admirable job succeeding Ralph Latham in the spotless white and gold No. 28

Chevelle. But a freak late season accident at Whitewater Valley forced him to the sidelines, and Chandler needed a driver.

In late 1971 Gilbert replaced an injured Gene Petro in Morgan Chandler's Kentucky-based No. 28 Chevelle. Chandler is shown at right. (Photo by Steve Cottle, courtesy Bob Markos, National Dirt Late Model Hall of Fame)

"Ralph left to drive the Jim Cook ZERO Dodge," Chandler recalled decades later. "Gene Petro started driving for me. We did pretty good. Then, right at the end of 1971, Petro got hit by a car in the pits at White-water Valley and it broke his ankle. Earl Smith was there that night and drove and won the feature. That was the only time he drove for me. But he was moving to Alabama, so he couldn't drive [full time]. That's when Floyd Gilbert started driving for me.

The duo was immediately successful, winning features that September at Whitewater Valley Speedway and Clay City, plus running second at Glen Este to points rival John Mugavin.

That season's Chevelle had some handling issues, Chandler said, and they struggled to keep the car hooked up.

"We were at Russell Springs, Kentucky and blew a left rear tire. All we had was a bigger tire, so we put it on the left rear. Everybody told us not to do that, but that car took off," Chandler said in a 2018 interview.

Gilbert and Chandler finished second to Butterball Wooldridge when he picked up the $2,000 top prize at the Kentucky Dirt Track Championship race in Clay City on September 10. It was the largest payout in Kentucky dirt racing history at that time. Wooldridge qualified first and Gilbert second, with Floyd winning the four-car fast dash. Billy Teegarden was the early leader in the 100-lap main event, but Wooldridge passed him on lap thirteen. Floyd took over second place ten circuits later, but even the two red flags that bunched the field couldn't help him pass the No. 59 Chevelle. Wooldridge collected the cash as Floyd finished second, with West Virginia's Herk Harbour third, Bob Chandler fourth, and Jim Howard fifth in a star-studded 20-car field.

Floyd backed up a trophy dash win by nabbing a feature victory later that month at Whitewater Valley. Gilbert aced out second-place Teegarden, John Vallo, Bob Smith, and Baldy McLaren in the 24-car feature field.

Butterball won Clay City again September 24, but this time he was driving Gilbert's No. 11 Chevelle. Each won a trophy dash, and Floyd battled Wooldridge and the fog before wheeling Chandler's car to a second-place finish.

"I was driving for Chandler, and I didn't have a driver for my car at Clay City. And Butterball said, 'Let me drive that.' I didn't tell him that you better run second. Chandler and them got mad because Butterball went out and won the race," a laughing Floyd told DirtFans.com. "I ran second. Chandler and them got madder than hell. They said you don't bring that car to anywhere we are racing again. Butterball passed us all. He took the low groove and buried that gas pedal, and I don't think he let it up until the checkered flag dropped. But I had a hell of a motor in it."

Floyd scored nearly 40 feature victories in 1971, capturing track championships at Clay City, Bluestone, and Glen Este.

He may well have notched another win in the season finale at Bluestone, but things ended with a thud in the 50-lap Sunday afternoon feature.

The Gilbert and Chandler combination immediately went to victory lane at Whitewater Valley Speedway. (Courtesy Fremont Hall of Fame, Mid-American Racing News archives)

"I was running second, but I broke an axle and was just trying to hold on and finish second," Gilbert told the *Cincinnati Enquirer* the following spring. "I hit the guard rail, the car glanced off the guardrail across the track, and I had to stop. The car behind me hit me head on and wrecked the car."

CHAPTER 7:

The Golden Season

As the 1972 season dawned, Floyd Gilbert's expectations couldn't have been higher. Coming off a career-best year, he had an alliance with car owner Morgan Chandler who had created a sparkling new gold metalflake Chevelle with seemingly unlimited potential. Floyd turned 42 just two days before Christmas 1971, and boldly predicted to Chandler and anyone who would listen that he would celebrate by winning 42 feature races.

All that anticipation came to a grinding halt on the backstretch of Tri-County Speedway after a vicious crash left Floyd and the new car upside down. Once he was out, Floyd was transported to Bethesda North Hospital, where he was treated and released.

After weeks and weeks of thrashing to complete the race car, Chandler, crew chief Cecil Snell, and a handful of volunteers worked until 4:30 a.m. on April 2. In what might have been an omen, Chandler's hauler broke down; the team borrowed a trailer from sponsor Pat Curry, owner of Rural Auto Parts, to make the short tow north to West Chester, Ohio. A large crowd gathered in the pit area on that chilly Easter morning as the team carefully backed the immaculate machine onto the ground and warmed the engine.

It was a rare Tri-County appearance for Gilbert, but Chandler had enjoyed great recent success there, winning often with Ralph Latham and Gene Petro.

Gilbert qualified well and was running in the third spot on the first lap of the 25-lap late model feature. As the pack exited turn two, Gilbert tried to move up the track—but clipped the left front corner of fourth-place Don Lamb's fast-closing Chevelle. The contact sent Gilbert flipping end over end five times for about 100 yards, the length of the back straightaway. The car ground to a halt, landing on its top.

"It was very wild and nasty. You could hear and almost feel every bounce and gouge while mud and pieces went flying," John Campbell recalled in 2018. "I watched him grab the wheel, hunch his shoulders up, and duck his head downward, and it was on, as they say. You could see he already knew what was about to happen. It's very surprising he wasn't really hurt bad. I recall his forehead was a little bit bloody."

Former racer Gary Rice also witnessed the incident.

"Tri-County had that concrete wall and he got a tire up on that wall, and that rolled him over," Rice recalled in 2018. "It scared everybody because it looked like the cage gave, and it took a little bit to get him out. It was probably ten minutes to get him out."

Chandler said a photo shows the car was as high as the trees behind the backstretch guardrail.

"Everybody got to Floyd and they were trying to take his helmet off, and he yelled, 'You're pulling my ears off!' I knew he was all right," Chandler said.

Floyd told the *Cincinnati Enquirer* years later the wreck stunned him.

"I remember somehow I crawled out of the wreck, but I was in a daze," Gilbert said. "I woke up just as I was climbing into the ambulance. For some reason, the only thing I could say was 'Where's my billfold? Where's my billfold?' I had five hundred dollars in it." The wallet and money were later found safe in his truck.

Lamb blamed Gilbert for the incident.

"Floyd was low and I was high, and I shot off the corner, and I don't think he saw me," Lamb told *Cincinnati Enquirer* reporter Paul Ritter. "He wanted to get into the high groove, and he changed lanes too quick. He came right over my left front. I tried to stop, but I was right into the wall. I sure was glad to come off that wall. I was sorry to see what happened, but I just couldn't help it."

Gilbert offered a slightly different take on the event decades later, in an interview with J.T. LeFever of DirtFans.com.

"I destroyed it, thanks to Don Lamb," Gilbert said of the Chevelle. "He kind of nosed his nose in between me and the wall, and I couldn't move out because there was a car on the outside of me. Then a guy on the inside of me moved out; I moved out. I hit Don Lamb's bumper, front end hit the guardrail; I went as far as the wheel fence and landed upside down. Really, I guess it wasn't Don's fault; the car beside me left me with no choice."

Floyd Gilbert's mount for the 1972 season was Morgan Chandler's impeccably prepared 1972 Chevelle. Together they won 42 features. (Courtesy Fremont Hall of Fame, Mid-American Auto Racing News archives)

The incident marked Gilbert's second straight crash of a Chandler-prepared car, as he'd ended the 1971 season by wadding up the previous No. 28 Chevelle in Bluestone Speedway's season finale.

"That really made me feel bad," Gilbert later told *Cincinnati Enquirer* reporter Webb Mathews. "I'm not one to tear up cars, and there I wrecked two in a row. But the crew had it in better shape than it had been at first in two weeks, and they had enough confidence in me to let me drive it again."

Decades later, Chandler recalled the car was a mess.

"We brought it home, got it off the truck, and the right front wheel didn't even touch the ground," he said.

They used a Porta-Power hydraulic tool to straight the frame and iron out the creases. Floyd returned to the track in late April at the re-configured 3/8-mile Whitewater Valley Speedway, and promptly went to victory lane.

The team began winning close to Floyd's Lockland, Ohio home, scor-ing three victories in three nights. On Friday May 5, Gilbert captured the checkers in a 25-lap feature at the newly reopened 3/8-mile North-ern Kentucky Speedway in Florence. A trip to Whitewater Valley Speed-way in southern Indiana produced another win, over Gerald Dixon and Pat Patrick, and a new track record of 17.54 seconds. On that Sunday night, Gilbert set fast time and then passed early leader Don Lamb on lap eleven to take a lead he wouldn't relinquish to win the season open-ing 25-lap feature at Ohio's Glen Este Speedway. John Mugavin wound up second, and Baldy McLaren was third.

Floyd made regular visits to the winner's circles at WVS and Glen Este, including winning for the seventh straight time at Glen Este May 21—a streak extending back to 1971—by outrunning Rodney Combs, John Mugavin, Larry Moore, and Nick Longano.

"You say 'I can win them all,' but that's not possible," Floyd told the *Cincinnati Enquirer* of his win streak. "Sooner or later, someone's going to beat you. But that's the kind of confidence you have to have if you're going to win a race."

Gilbert (No. 28) races with Ohio's Steve Edmisten (No. 7) at Glen Este Speedway. Gilbert captured nine victories and his third straight Glen Este championship that season. (Courtesy Fremont Hall of Fame, Mid-American Auto Racing News archives)

A creature of habit, Floyd admitted in that *Enquirer* story that he liked to arrive at Glen Este at about 1 a.m. from wherever he'd raced Saturday night to prepare for the next race.

"There's no one around here then, and it's nice," Floyd said. "I walk around, study the race track, and get some sleep under that shade tree."

The winning streak also included Whitewater's 50-lap invitational race June 6, when Floyd came from the back of the pack to outrun Rodney Combs. Add in a June 9 victory at Clay City, Kentucky that pushed the win total to nine. It reached ten the following night when Gilbert bombed his old record, setting a new mark of 17.037 seconds and handily winning for the fourth time at Whitewater Valley—a feat that made the Associated Press wire and was reported nationwide.

After arguments with drivers and complaints about the surface, maverick Tri-County promoter Bill Redwine covered his track's dirt surface with asphalt at the end of May 1972. This ultimately prompted Northern Kentucky promoters to jump to Saturday nights, since so many Cincinnati-area cars were competing Fridays at Clay City.

While he often made winning look easy, Floyd barely claimed his twelfth victory of the season June 17 at Whitewater Valley's Pepsi Twin 50s because a "fist-sized rock" flew into the cockpit of his race-leading

Chevelle with only a couple laps to go. The rock shattered his bubble face shield, bloodied his nose, and nearly knocked him unconscious. After a momentary bobble, he recovered and held off rivals Gene Petro and Pat Patrick, despite blood streaming down his face. Gilbert wiped off the blood and accepted the checkered flag but was then rushed to a nearby hospital where he was treated and released.

"If it hadn't been for that [shield] when I got hit in the nose at Whitewater, it would have probably took my nose and head off," Floyd told DirtFans.com. "That rock was a pound and three quarter. It hit the screen, the steering wheel, and hit my nose. I had to catch myself; I started to falling over. I had one more lap to go and made it. I won the race and pulled in the infield. It was a special race, paying a few bucks more. So, I want to go to the hospital, blood just pouring out of my nose. They said, 'Here, wipe off; we have to take these pictures first.' So, we took the pictures then they took me to the hospital. But it didn't break my nose."

Car owner/builder Morgan Chandler (left) and Floyd Gilbert were virtually unbeatable during the 1972 season, combining to win 42 feature races at tracks in Indiana, Kentucky and Ohio. (Courtesy Fremont Hall of Fame, Mid-American Auto Racing News archives)

A week later the team swept the weekend, winning at Clay City, WVS, and Glen Este. The Sunday triumph was notable; Floyd survived a record eleven red flags in Glen Este's June 25 feature to notch his fifth win there. Baldy McLaren ran second in the Earl's Towing Chevelle.

Gilbert wrapped up the month of June with his sixteenth victory and a $1,000 payday by dominating a 50-lap feature on the Clay City half-mile. Gilbert started on the outside of the front row, immediately took the lead from fast qualifier Billy Teegarden, and led every lap. Teegarden chased Floyd in a jolly game of follow-the-leader before his car overheated late in the going. Gerald Dixon finished second and Billy faded to third.

Gilbert and Chandler claimed a $1,000 payday the following night at Whitewater Valley's 76-lap feature but didn't enter the 76-lap Sunday night show at Glen Este, where John Mugavin won.

Gilbert rebounded by again winning five straight, sweeping Clay City, Whitewater Valley, and Glen Este July 7-9, which included edging out Teegarden for his eighth win in ten starts at WVS. By mid-July, Floyd held a 99-point lead over Pat Patrick at WVS, with Gene Petro, Billy Teegarden, and Baldy McLaren filling out the top five positions.

The next weekend, the team again won Clay City on Friday, captured a 100-lap feature at Whitewater Valley, and then towed all night to Pennsboro, West Virginia for an all-star show.

"We had some mighty tough competition and finished third," he told the *Enquirer* the following month. "But we had to drive all night to get there. I fell asleep in my race car waiting for the feature to start." Gilbert wasn't enamored with the legendary 5/8-mile Ritchie County Speedway oval.

"It used to be an old fairgrounds track. You fall into a narrow turn with sand in it at a hundred or a hundred and ten miles an hour, and if you can visualize what it's like to go suddenly from pavement that's dry to a part that's got ice on it... Well, you know what that's like," Gilbert related. "At first it wasn't much fun, but about halfway through I got the feel of it."

Coming off two straight 100-lap races, Floyd suffered his costliest loss of the year the following Friday, when the engine in Chandler's Chevelle failed after leading the first 68 laps of Clay City's $1,000-to-win Mid-Season Championship. It would be his lone loss there all year.

Gilbert got on the phone and arranged to drive a 1965 Chevelle owned by John Holmes, which he promptly wheeled to victory the following night at Whitewater Valley. He ran fourth that Sunday at Glen Este as Billy Teegarden won his second race of the weekend after taking Northern Kentucky's first Saturday night show.

At the end of July, Gilbert and Chandler traveled to Mansfield, Ohio, where they dominated the 50-lap invitational race. Floyd took the lead from Ron Dolen and then ran a "near flawless" race, turning back local stars Dorus Wisecarver and Dolen, according to the Mansfield newspaper.

"We made it a weekend trip," Gilbert told the *Cincinnati Enquirer's* Webb Mathews. "I got spun out twice Saturday night and finished sixth. But Sunday night we ran away and hid."

Gilbert said the Mansfield oval was built almost like a small version of the Indianapolis speedway, with four distinct corners. "It's like a long square with a slight straight between each corner. It's dirt, but it gets hard and black just like asphalt," he said.

The Mansfield win and its $1,000 payday signaled the start of ten feature victories in a dozen starts and fifteen wins in seventeen races between July 28 and September 8, a stretch that included winning the 100-lap Indiana State Championship at Whitewater, where Floyd outran Gene Petro, Pat Patrick and Paul "Butterball" Wooldridge.

Two weeks later, Floyd led all 100 laps to dominate Northern Kentucky's Mid-Season Championship race. He pocketed $1,000 for the victory over Wooldridge and Baldy McLaren.

"The track was in beautiful condition at Northern," Floyd told reporters after the August 19 victory. "I've never seen it that good since it opened."

That stretch included three rainouts at Clay City, which—given the team's nearly unbeatable record there—could easily have been three more victories.

The only races that Gilbert entered but failed to win that month came August 12 at Whitewater Valley, which was won by Vern LeFevers, and the race on August 27, when he battled Ford racer Ron Baker for the checkered flag in a Sunday night show at Glen Este. Gilbert passed Baker with two laps remaining, but then the caution flag immediately flew for a spin, meaning the running order reverted to the last completed lap, a common practice at most short tracks. That awarded the top spot back to Baker, who withstood a furious charge from Gilbert on the tight quarter-mile oval.

The Gilbert-Chandler combination reeled off three more victories on Labor Day weekend, including a $1,000 payday for a Clay City 50-lap test over Jim Patrick and another 100-lap showdown at Whitewater Valley; the twenty-car field was fully inverted, and fastest qualifier Gilbert stormed from the back into the lead by lap eleven. Floyd put the entire field at least a lap down, with Chick Hale holding on for second and Vern LeFevers third.

Besides a trophy and a checkered flag, victory lane also included the presentation of a framed charcoal portrait of Floyd, drawn by local artist Sandy Cox.

The weekend concluded with a Sunday night victory in the 50-lap Glen Este feature, his seventh of the season there and 35th overall. After qualifying fastest and winning the fast dash, Gilbert spun early in the feature and went to the rear of the field before charging to the front and taking the top spot on lap 26. He led the rest of the way, besting second-place Nick Longano by a half-lap to take the top prize and his third straight Glen Este track championship.

The team won once more at Clay City—after wrapping up that track title weeks before - and twice more at Glen Este. With Clay City closing in early September, Gilbert and Chandler found a new Friday night playground by capturing the first of two straight wins at the all new Ponderosa Speedway south of Danville, Kentucky, a high-banked dirt oval dubbed the "Little Daytona."

With an estimated 3,600 fans looking on, Gilbert qualified first at sixteen seconds flat, started on the pole and laid the wood to a strong field on Ponderosa's opening night. He was a half-lap ahead by the mid-way point of the 50-lap feature. A caution for an Eddie Carrier spin bunched the field and gave second-place Butterball Wooldridge an opportunity, but Gilbert wasted no time extending his lead again.

Floyd Gilbert (No. 28) passing early race leader Dick DeBolt (No. 91) to claim his second straight feature at Ponderosa Speedway in September 1972. (Photo by Steve Cottle, courtesy Fremont Hall of Fame, Mid-American Auto Racing News archives)

The following weekend, Ponderosa's fourteen-car feature field was completely inverted, with third-fastest qualifier Gilbert rolling off from the twelfth starting spot. He worked through traffic, passed then-leader Dick DeBolt on lap sixteen, and rolled to victory in the 50-lap show. DeBolt finished second, driving a winged 1968 Camaro owned by Gene Petro; another Indiana racer, Tommy Day, came in third in his winged six-cylinder Chevy II.

Those victories cemented Floyd's initial Ponderosa Speedway track title.

Gilbert was among the favorites for a one-off 200-lap race billed in advertisements as the 1972 Dirt Track World Championship at Kentucky International Raceway: a flat, 5/8-mile former horse track located a few miles from Florence Kentucky. The race, which some media accounts branded the Bluegrass World Series, was the brainchild of some first-time Cincinnati area promoters who hoped to attract drivers from ARCA, USAC, and possibly NASCAR to race for $4,000 to win. They leased the track, which had been idle for three seasons but had previously hosted ARCA and USAC races.

Days of rain before the race made the surface a mess, and the relatively large, hearty crowd had to endure a slowly run program in chilly, windy conditions, and long lines at the few open concession stands and restrooms. NASCAR star Lee Roy Yarbrough blew up two engines in two different cars attempting to qualify and missed the program.

Yarbrough wound up in Floyd's motorhome on Saturday, Chandler recalled, and they all wound up at Northern Kentucky Speedway.

"He [Yarbrough] said those cars were running way faster than they should, and people were sticking their hands through the fence cheering them on. He said it was the craziest thing he'd ever seen," Chandler said.

Sunday's "race" featured little passing, fourteen yellow flags and ninety laps run under caution. The race stopped once for the lone ambulance on the property to take an expectant mother to a local hospital and resumed once it returned.

Pennsylvania pro Bob Wearing was the fastest qualifier at 30.008 seconds and led the first 74 laps before Floyd steered Chandler's Chevelle to the top spot. His time there was short-lived, however, as a lapped car pulled into his path, wrecking the car and Floyd's visions of the $4,000 payday. Wearing took the lead on the restart and led the rest of the way, claiming victory in his battered Camaro. Veteran Ralph "Pappy" Clary finished second, Billy Teegarden was third in his 1965 Chevelle. With darkness falling and only ten cars still running, the race was flagged complete after 182 laps.

Gilbert had to wait until the following weekend to make good on his pre-season boast of winning 42 times in Chandler's Chevelle. He took the checkers in Northern Kentucky Speedway's 50-lap season finale but fell short of the track championship, which went to Billy Teegarden. Floyd started ninth in the 24-car field and powered into the lead by lap 23. Afterward he held up four fingers on his right hand

and two on his left for a black and white Steve Cottle photograph that memorialized the accomplishment.

Prior to the season, 42-year-old Floyd Gilbert predicted he would win 42 features in Morgan Chandler's car. He finally earned that forty-second victory Oct. 7 at Northern Kentucky Speedway. (Photo by Steve Cottle, courtesy Fremont Hall of Fame, Mid-American Auto Racing News archives)

In addition, he scored seven other wins in three other cars to total 49 victories in just over sixty starts. That win total was second best in the nation for 1972, exceeded only by asphalt star Dick Trickle's 67 feature wins. But as Gilbert often reminded people, it took Trickle more than 100 starts to rack up that many victories.

The team finished with track championships at Clay City, Glen Este, Ponderosa, and Whitewater Valley—the most ever by one driver and one team in a single season in the Tri-State region. They also finished eighth in points at Northern Kentucky.

But why were they so dominant? Floyd said the car "drove like a Cadillac."

"Floyd was really on his game that year," Chandler said. "It didn't matter how slick the track got, that car got faster."

Most tracks ran open competition rules back then, meaning the engine could be all you could stuff beneath the hood. Chandler's engines began as 454s, but mostly ran 486 cubic inches in the Chevelle, and some were over 500 cubic inches, making 700 horsepower. The car often ran with two Holley carburetors atop a Weiand tunnel ram intake manifold, much like Pro Stock drag racers of that era. This setup added another seventy horsepower.

Chandler was also working with 180-degree exhaust headers, which widened the engine's torque range. NASCAR's Junior Johnson employed the same technology that season on his cars, driven by Bobby Allison.

Decades later, Chandler offered a more detailed explanation of some of his speed secrets.

"We had a lot of horsepower—which helped at Clay City with those long straightaways—but a lot of people thought that was all we had. But the chassis worked good too," Chandler said. The 3,500-pound car utilized stock Chevrolet front suspension, while the rear suspension included coil springs and a panhard bar to keep the massive rear tires planted.

"That car had a narrowed rear end. We ran a quick change [differential], but instead of thirty-two-inch axles, it had twenty-eight-inch axles. I thought it would get better traction off the turn, something from my drag racing days. It seemed to work real good," Chandler revealed. But the tricks weren't confined to the suspension, and anyone who carefully examined the gold beast—either live or in photographs—will attest.

"The rule was the front spark plug could only be two inches behind the centerline of the ball joint. You couldn't move the motor back, so I moved the body back five inches. You know how the [front] bumper would curve around the side, we had to cut that off because it kept hitting the front wheels. It was a 'Funny Car' dragster that learned to turn corners," Chandler said.

CHAPTER 8:

Split Leads to
Duncan's Delight

Floyd traveled to Toledo, Ohio, January 13, 1973, to accept the inaugural *Mid-American Auto Racing News* Feature Winner Award during the publication's annual promoter's workshop.

Building on the success of their spectacular 1972 season, Chandler and his crew constructed a sparkling new Camaro with dreams of continuing to dominate regional short tracks. While there was nothing mechanically wrong with the Chevelle that some new sheet metal couldn't fix, Chandler felt the lighter Camaro, when paired with one of his massive Chevrolet engines, would be all but unbeatable.

The new car debuted sitting still at the Cincinnati Cavalcade of Customs auto show in January 1973 and won an award for the two-tone gold metalflake and maroon paint lovingly sprayed by Roy Lee Bell of Dixie Auto Body. The following year, Chevrolet used a nearly identical two-tone styling treatment on its Rally Sport model Camaros.

In a story in *Inside Kentucky Sports* magazine, Gilbert told writer Jim Wills "It's awfully hard not to brag on what we have done or what we will do. But being with such a tremendous garage as I am, we will shoot for fifty feature wins and maybe settle for forty-three."

Anticipation ran high for the 1973 season, as car builder Morgan Chandler and Gilbert debuted a sleek new 1973 Camaro. But Floyd didn't like how the Camaro handled and they split after a couple of months. (Mike Roland photo, courtesy DirtFans.com)

Sponsors Rural Auto Parts, Jeff Williams Boron Distributing, and Kendall GT-1 oil were back in place and everything appeared ready for another landmark season. But it wasn't to be.

"Floyd drove the Camaro one time, wrecked, and wouldn't drive it again," Chandler said.

Floyd began the year the way he finished 1972, with back-to-back wins, taking an Eldora Speedway late model feature in the year-old Chevelle on April 15 and winning another 25-lapper at Whitewater Valley the following weekend, where he started twelfth and took the lead on lap fourteen, holding off Vern LeFevers and John Mugavin at the checkers. He then won at Lawrenceburg, Indiana—after the promoter bet him he couldn't.

Decades later, Chandler admitted the Camaro might have been a mistake.

"We built the Camaro. I don't know; we probably shouldn't have. The Camaro had a tubular chassis. Floyd drove it one night and wouldn't drive it anymore," Chandler said. "We still had the Chevelle. He got Bill

Teegarden to drive the Camaro. I didn't want to run both all the time, so I told Floyd we would just run the Chevelle and keep the Camaro for a spare. Which should have made him happy, but he promised Teegarden he could drive it. We ran them both for a while. Teegarden and Floyd fell out. Teegarden was letting Floyd win, but one time got mad because he passed him. Teegarden pulled up beside him on the last turn and backed off."

In late May, despite Gilbert winning five races in his first ten starts, the previous season's dominant team split up.

In a June 3, 1973, interview with the *Cincinnati Enquirer*, Gilbert described the situation as "awful touchy."

"I can't get a whole lot of animosity started. I would rather leave things as they are; we parted friends," Gilbert said. "This disagreement has been arising for about a month or six weeks and it just came to a head last Monday. I can't say I'm totally disappointed. Racing had got to be so cotton-picking involved it just wasn't fun anymore."

More than 25 years later, Gilbert was a bit more forthcoming in a Dirtfans.com interview.

"In 1973 they built a new Camaro; I drove it and won with it. But I said it don't handle and I didn't want to drive it, so they put Billy Teegarden in it," Gilbert recalled in the DirtFans.com interview. "We run first and second over at Northern Kentucky [Florence Speedway]; so, they want Billy. They want someone to drive the Camaro. They ended up selling the Chevelle [some time] after they fired me."

In a follow-up June 1973 newspaper story, Teegarden said his stint with Chandler was originally expected to be "just temporary," but they had so much success he was soon leading the points standings at Northern Kentucky Speedway, home track for both Chandler and Teegarden. That same article noted that Chandler immediately hired veteran Pat Patrick to drive the Chevelle. The writer dubbed that arrangement a "super team" after both scored early victories. But it lasted only a few weeks before Ralph Latham—one of Chandler's former drivers who graduated to ARCA and USAC stock car competition—agreed to run some races in Chandler's cars, leaving Patrick looking for a ride.

In the June 3 newspaper story, Gilbert described a race car he'd purchased from Nick Longano, along with brothers John and Allen Miller, another he could drive. He then offered a tantalizing glimpse into the future.

"I talked to a man down in Lexington, Kentucky. He's a millionaire, so you can see why I'd want to drive for him," Floyd said, never mentioning R.L. Duncan's name but it was easy to read between the lines.

Floyd soldiered on in that serviceable equipment, qualifying first at Whitewater Valley, finishing second at Glen Este in a Chevelle borrowed from John Holmes of Valley Radiator Service, and third behind Patrick in his former ride. He won at Whitewater Valley in the Chevelle he and the Millers owned, then won again at WVS over Ron Edwards and Vern LeFevers on June 23. That same night at Northern, Teegarden outran Patrick as the Chandler Chevys finished first and second, with Gene Petro third.

The following night, Floyd finished second overall in Glen Este Speedway's Quarter-Mile Dirt Track Championship race, posting a third-place run in the first 50-lap feature to go with a fourth-place effort in the second segment. Pat Patrick made his first appearance of the year there in the Chandler Chevelle and won the first segment over Jim Curry, who won the overall title, and Gilbert. Patrick broke in the second 50-lapper.

It was a challenging, humbling time for the proud, confident Gilbert. "I'd go to the track with my helmet in my hand, looking for a ride," Floyd later reflected to the *Cincinnati Enquirer* in an August interview.

But fate was about to intervene in the form of that Kentucky millionaire. The deal to drive for R.L. Duncan in a car prepared by brothers Logan and Charles Grider came together around Independence Day.

"I'll never forget when I got the call to drive for Duncan," Gilbert told DirtFans.com. "I got a surprise; I was at home and I got a call from Logan [Grider]. He said, 'Do you want to drive for us?' I said, 'Oh yeah.' Ain't many times anybody beat fifty-nine when Butterball [Wooldridge] was driving it. So, I stepped into that; I didn't even have a ride. Then I said, 'Anytime you can bring twenty-eight here, I'll run rings around it.' But I felt that because it [Duncan's] was a lot better car."

After driving several different cars, Gilbert settled into the seat of the Duncan's De-light Chevelle in July 1973 at Ponderosa Speedway in Kentucky. (Courtesy Fremont Hall of Fame, Mid-American Auto Racing News archives)

The Duncan team was just a few months into David Speer's tenure replacing Wooldridge. Speer earned many wins at Ponderosa Speedway and Richmond Raceway in Richmond, Kentucky, including June 29, when he came from the tail to claim the lead on lap fourteen and win the 40-lap race. But the team still opted to make the mid-season switch.

Floyd's first start for Duncan came at Ponderosa on July 6. After setting fast time, Gilbert was leading the 60-lap feature race when a me-chanical failure sent the car hard into the outside guardrail.

A rejuvenated Gilbert wheeled his own Chevelle to a second-place finish the following night at Northern Kentucky, and a win on Sunday night at Glen Este Speedway.

The Grider brothers had Duncan's Chevelle as good as new the follow-ing weekend, and Gilbert was leading the 60-lap feature at Lake Cumber-land Sportsdrome near Somerset, Kentucky, when fate intervened again. On the final lap, a slower car spun just in front of Gilbert, forcing him to dive low toward the infield. Gerald Dixon slipped past for the lead and the win, while Gilbert recovered to finish second.

His first victory for Duncan came July 20 in a 40-lap feature at Ponderosa. After starting eleventh, Floyd had to work his way through traffic to catch early race leader Ray Cash. By the twenty-fifth circuit, he was on the rear bumper of Cash's dark red Camaro. After several laps threading their way through slower traffic, Cash slipped high in turn two as Gilbert claimed the lead and the win. Cash finished second, and Dale Clary was third.

Floyd hopped back into his own car for a July 22 runner-up to John Mugavin at Glen Este.

The Gilbert-Duncan combination really picked up steam the following weekend. Floyd won Ponderosa's 60-lap Mid-Season championship feature race, taking the lead from Fats Coffey on lap 22 and holding off a furious charge from fastest qualifier Billy Teegarden, in the Morgan Chandler Chevelle. This despite Gilbert's engine sputtering noticeably, and running the final three laps with a rapidly deflating right rear tire.

After a mediocre finish at Northern the next night, Floyd rebounded to score his twelfth victory of the season in the 100-lap Mid-Season championship at Glen Este on July 29, a race that attracted a track record 43 late models for the $1,000 top prize.

"It's a jewel of a race car," Gilbert said of the Duncan Chevelle after the Glen Este win, adding it was comparable to Chandler's mighty mount of 1972. After setting fast time, Gilbert battled with outside pole sitter John Mugavin for much of the race's first 67 circuits. Once he passed Mugavin's Camaro, Gilbert stretched the margin to a full straightaway. Following second-place Mugavin were Pat Patrick, who was driving Gilbert's Chevelle, Jim Curry, and Tommy Day.

The following weekend, Floyd claimed a $1,200 payday by earning the pole and holding off Vern LeFevers, Ron Edwards, Pat Patrick and Chick Hale to win the 50-lap Indiana Dirt Track Championship at Whitewater Valley on August 4. The top-finishing duo was pictured on the following week's cover of Mid-American Auto Racing News, clutching giant trophies.

Floyd Gilbert (right) outran Vern LeFevers (left) to win the 1973 Indiana State Championship. This image, with trophy queen Nina Stainbrook, appeared on the cover of *Mid-American Auto Racing News*. (Photo by Stan Jeffrey, courtesy Fremont Hall of Fame, Mid-American Auto Racing News archives)

Floyd collected another checkered flag August 17, wheeling the Duncan Chevelle to victory at Ponderosa Speedway over fast qualifier Butterball Wooldridge, Fats Coffey, Gerald Dixon, and fast dash winner E.M. Snowden Jr.

He strung together three straight wins at Ponderosa during this stretch, including a 30-lap battle with top qualifier Butterball Wooldridge in the E.T. Morse Monte Carlo. Gilbert pulled away in the final ten laps to take the win. Wooldridge wound up second, and Fats Coffey was third.

Perhaps Floyd's most impressive Ponderosa run was August 24, when he started on the last row of the twenty-car field and roared into the lead by lap ten. Things got interesting on lap 38, when the car's accelerator hung up entering turn one. Floyd clobbered the wall, but he was able to limp home for the win ahead of E.M. Snowden Jr., and Gerald Dixon.

Gilbert ended the month by winning the Pepsi 100 at Glen Este on August 26. A story in *Mid-American Auto Racing News* declared "when it comes to winning the big ones, there's just no denying 'Flying Floyd' Gilbert, the 43-year-old 'king of the dirt tracks' in this area." Floyd had to work traffic, coming through the pack to take the lead on lap 51. Late in the going, he fended off a challenge from Charlie Swartz.

Floyd kept the heat on in September, qualifying first and running second to William "Fats" Coffey at Ponderosa, setting a new track record at Northern before breaking an axle—but coming back on Sunday night to win another 100-lap show at Glen Este.

Coffey withstood fastest qualifier Gilbert's best charge to win Ponderosa on September 7, in a race that writer Jim Wills described as "one of the most thrilling events of the season." Both started at the rear of the twelve-car field but worked their way into the lead by lap six. From there the two future Hall of Fame drivers ran bumper-to-bumper for more than thirty laps. Gerald Dixon got by Gilbert on lap 38, but then spun out on the final circuit. Floyd salvaged second, and David Speer finished third in Dale Napper's Camaro.

Back at Northern Kentucky Speedway on September 8, Floyd established a new track qualifying record but couldn't translate that speed into a win. Billy Teegarden set the record in Morgan Chandler's Camaro at 19.31 seconds, only to have Gilbert snatch it away at 19.30. An accident took Teegarden out of contention and Floyd was running a solid second to race leader Bubby James when an axle broke on lap 21. Ron Edwards and John Mugavin passed the slowing red Chevelle, but Gilbert wrestled it home in fourth place, just ahead of Chuck McWilliams.

Floyd was pictured in *Inside Kentucky Sports* magazine for the second time in 1973, smiling from the seat of the Duncan Chevelle while clutching a checkered flag. In the accompanying Jim Wills story about race tracks in central Kentucky, Gilbert was cited as a regular contender at Ponderosa and Northern Kentucky.

A September 9 victory at Glen Este finally propelled Gilbert into the track points lead—a spot he'd been striving for all season—and prompted rival John Mugavin to all but give up on winning his hometown track's title.

"About the only way I could win the championship there now would be if Floyd dropped dead today, and I won everything else at the track," Mugavin told the *Cincinnati Enquirer*.

Gilbert returned to victory lane September 22 at Northern Kentucky after early leader Chuck McWilliams blew a tire on his Chevelle and took out 100 feet of guardrail. Floyd temporarily lost the Glen Este points lead in mid-September but held a slim margin over rival Ron Baker entering that track's final race on Sunday September 30.

Altogether, Floyd racked up more than forty victories in 1973 by the time the attention of the dirt late model community shifted to Earl Baltes' Eldora Speedway and the third annual World 100, also on September 30. Nestled among the cornfields near the Ohio-Indiana border, Eldora was a brutally fast high-banked half-mile clay oval that Baltes touted as "Auto racing's showcase" and the Midwest's fastest dirt track.

The World 100 was its preeminent event. The 100-lap test was called the World's 100 at that time, and winners were dubbed World's Champion. It formally started in 1971 with a then-unheard-of payout of $4,000 to win, and the victor's check rose by $1,000 each year. Bruce Gould won the inaugural race and United States Auto Club standout Verlin Eaker pocketed $5,000 for his 1972 win.

CHAPTER 9:

Winning the World 100

Baseball historians have long debated whether Babe Ruth really pointed at the fence in the third game of the 1932 World Series and predicted he would send a home run over the outfield wall. But there is no question Flyin' Floyd Gilbert called his shot in the 1973 World 100, telling two competitors the precise lap in which he would take the lead, and how he would emerge victorious.

After 140 of the nation's best cars and drivers completed qualifying, Floyd and the R.L. Duncan Chevelle registered the third quickest time, trailing only Billy Teegarden in the Chandler Camaro and Michigan pavement star Bob Senneker.

Among those failing to make the 22-car starting lineup were NAS-CAR Grand American champion and former Daytona 500 winner Dewayne "Tiny" Lund, Ralph Latham, and defending World 100 champion Verlin Eaker, who won the B-main.

Once all the heat races were completed and the feature lineup was assembled on the Eldora Speedway frontstretch, track champion Gene Petro would start on the pole with fellow Indiana driver and late model rookie Roger Grossnickle to his outside. Rodney Combs lined up outside of row two with Gilbert on the inside. Senneker lined up behind Gilbert in fifth, and fast qualifier Teegarden started behind Combs in sixth.

"Gene and I were standing there talking when Floyd walked up," Grossnickle recalled in a 2018 interview. "I didn't know him. He looked at me and said something about it looked like one of my tires was losing air. Then he said, 'You won't lead.' He looked at Gene and said, 'I'll let you lead the first thirteen laps, and then old Floyd is gonna go right on by.' Then he turned and walked away."

It played out just that way.

When the green flag waved, Grossnickle and Petro drag raced to the first turn, with Petro leading down the back straightaway. Floyd passed Grossnickle for second, and the trio separated itself from the rest of the pack.

"We kind of pulled away, and for some reason, I was counting the laps every time we went past the flag stand. Now, why was I counting the laps? What Floyd said was in my head," Grossnickle admitted. "Floyd passed me and on the fourteenth lap. Floyd passed Gene, just like he said he would, and went on and won. That is a true story. He flat called it."

When Petro's Camaro slipped up the track in turn four of lap thirteen, Gilbert pulled even at the start-finish line. The two warriors briefly touched entering turn one, with Gilbert's red Chevelle recovering first and squirting into the lead on lap fourteen, just as predicted.

"Petro got a bit high coming out of the fourth turn," Dan Heath wrote in the April 1974 issue of *Stock Car Racing* magazine. "With Petro's loss of traction, Gilbert pulled alongside. As both cars powered side by side down the front straight, the crowd jumped to their feet to see which one, if either, would make it through turn one... For one horrifying moment, it appeared as if both cars might hurtle over the guardrail—or worse, both might spin and block the track in front of the fast approaching pack. Only deft driving by these two skillful competitors averted a disaster."

Unbeknownst to Grossnickle, Gilbert nearly orchestrated his own shot in qualifying.

"Floyd raised sandbagging to an art form. Back then, you got in line when you wanted to. I walked by and asked him if he wasn't gonna qualify," veteran Larry Moore recalled in a 2017 interview. "He just said,

'No, I'm waiting for this track to get right so I can start on the front row.' They were gonna invert six, so he wanted to time in fifth or sixth, so he could start on the front row."

Gilbert posted the fastest qualifying time for much of the session before being surpassed by Teegarden and Senneker, ultimately timing in third quickest among cars from ten states and Canada; just one second separated the fastest car from the slowest.

In his *Stock Car Racing* magazine story Heath reported, "Railbirds picked Floyd Gilbert, winner of 43 feature wins on dirt tracks in Kentucky, Ohio, and Indiana as the man to beat."

Once Floyd took the race lead, he used the upper groove and began putting car after car a lap down.

Floyd Gilbert (No. 59) uses the high groove to pass Iowa's Ed Sanger (No. 95) en route to winning the 1973 World 100 at Eldora Speedway. Thirty-one years later he and Sanger were inducted into the Hall of Fame on the same day. (John Butler photo)

Friend and rival Gene Petro (No. 90) started on the World 100 pole but lost the lead and the race to Gilbert (No. 59), who is shown here putting Petro a lap down. (John Butler photo)

The pack ran nose-to-tail for several laps, but when Grossnickle bobbled on lap forty, it opened the door for Teegarden, who charged from fifth to third. When the crossed flags appeared at lap fifty, Gilbert held a straightaway lead over second-place Petro, with Teegarden a close third.

Ten laps later, Teegarden powered past Petro's white Camaro for second—but Gilbert had checked out. With thirty laps remaining he had lapped all but the second, third, and fourth-place machines of Teegarden, Petro, and Rodney Combs. That became two when Combs pulled his ailing Chevelle into the pits with fuel pump failure.

Decades later, Chandler remembers the one that got away.

"Billy got to second, but by then Floyd had a half-lap lead. We didn't get a caution, so we didn't get a chance to race him," Chandler recalled.

A half-lap behind with twenty circuits remaining, Teegarden began pushing his Camaro even harder, trying to reel in Gilbert's streaking Chevelle. On the sport's biggest stage, Floyd dashed beneath the checkered flag about half a lap in front of his former teammate and the car he'd refused to drive.

What was it that Gilbert told crew chief Logan Grider back in the summer? "Anytime you can bring twenty-eight here, I'll run rings around it."

Nearly five decades of World 100s later, Gilbert's win remains among the most dominant performances in race history, trailing Donnie Moran in 1989 and Billy Moyer's 1991 showings, when each driver lapped the entire field.

Gilbert and Duncan collected a $6,000 payday plus $870 lap money for leading 87 circuits. Teegarden earned $1,500 for second place, the only other car on the lead lap. Petro finished third, one lap down, 1971 World 100 winner Bruce Gould finished fourth in his Joey Stricker-owned Ford Torino, and Indiana's Dick DeBolt was fifth. Rounding out the top ten were Grossnickle, who was running out of fuel; Chuck McWilliams, who had recovered from an early spin; Michigan's Frank Lamp, who started shotgun on the field; Dave Chase, and Chick Hale.

Floyd Gilbert (left) is all smiles as he clutches the prestigious World 100 globe trophy. Also pictured are chief mechanic Logan Grider (center) and Eldora Speedway owner Earl Baltes. (John Butler photo)

After hoisting the iconic globe trophy and hurriedly posing for photographs, Gilbert didn't stick around. As he told DirtFans.com, there was another race to win.

"I had one thing in mind, and that was to get out of there and head to Glen Este Speedway to win the points championship for the fourth consecutive year. Which I also won the feature that night at Glen Este," Gilbert said, adding at the time that championship meant more than winning Eldora.

"I didn't really have time to consider what I had done at Eldora. I just got my twenty-two-hundred-dollar cut, and away we headed to Glen Este. There was no drinking of a glass of wine or anything; fact is, we counted the money out in the parking lot. There was no big hullabaloo or anything. Common situation. Nothing thrilling; no big deal about it."

Instead Gilbert hopped into a waiting Chevy El Camino driven by John Miller and headed south for the roughly two-hour drive to Cincinnati's east side.

"We got there at eight twenty-five p.m. and my son, David, had my car running and the gear changed and ready to go and we went racing," Gilbert recalled. Since he arrived too late to qualify, Gilbert started last in the fifteen-car field. But he passed Bruce Merz for the lead on lap 21, then won the feature and the track championship. "There wasn't nothing going to slow me down that day," he told DirtFans.com.

Longtime friend, crew member and race official Mike Roland described Gilbert's double that day as the "most amazing thing" he'd ever seen.

"He drove the Flyin' Two that was owned by Bill Sallee, from Erlanger, Kentucky. Now this is the funny part," Roland recalled. "That car was Morgan's [Chandler] old Chevelle that he sold to Bill. It was the car that Floyd drove to forty-two feature wins in seventy-two. When Morgan sold that car to Bill it was on the condition that Floyd was not to drive it. Well, Floyd worked something out with Bill, and the rest is history."

The celebration came later.

"I had more fun that night at the bar there right near [racer] Johnny Mugavin. When we won and left Glen Este, we went there and threw a hundred dollars down and I said drink it up, everybody! And we drank it up. I had twenty-two hundred dollars from Eldora, and three hundred from Glen Este. No, wait a minute; I gave a hundred and fifty dollars back to Ron Baker. I gave him half of it because I hit him and spun him. But his car didn't finish anyway, so I probably should have saved the money."

Decades later, internationally renowned racing artist Roger Warrick perfectly captured that day's escapades with a caricature, showing Gilbert's aviator sunglasses reflecting checkered flags as he wheeled the Duncan Chevelle, with World 100 trophy in the trunk, money flying out the back, and a green road sign pointing toward Glen Este Speedway.

Gilbert's landmark 1973 victory is also included in Bill Holder's 2013 book *Eldora Speedway: The History of the Most Famous Dirt Track in America 1954-2013*. Holder's book lists the World 100 finishes of all drivers, including Floyd, and documents another major victory which occurred just one week later.

FLOYD GILBERT
Lockland, Ohio
1973 World 100 Winner

Motorsports artist Roger Warrick captured the spirit of Floyd' Gilbert's career-defining World 100 victory and the Glen Este Speedway championship he secured later that same night. (Courtesy Roger Warrick)

CHAPTER 10:

Nearly Unbeatable

Winning dirt racing's biggest prize, more than forty-plus feature races, and two more track championships would be a career for some racers, but Floyd's 1973 season didn't end September 30 with the World 100/Glen Este double. Not when the Johnny Appleseed 150—another significant dirt late model race with a $10,000 total payout—was the following weekend at Mansfield, Ohio.

Coming off the World 100 and already the Mansfield track record holder at 21.35 seconds, Floyd was the clear favorite as more than 100 drivers entered to try and make the 28-car field. Entries included NASCAR star Tiny Lund, Kentucky's Butterball Wooldridge, Pennsylvania's Bob Wearing, Iowa's Ed Sanger, and dozens from racing hotbed northern Ohio, all gunning for the $1,700 top prize.

Floyd lived up to the advance press by qualifying first at 22.10. Lund then captured the Race of States, featuring the fastest qualifier from each state, where Gilbert ran fourth. Lund, an imposing six feet, five inches tall and 250 pounds, with a reputation of winning on dirt or pavement, soon became friends with Floyd. In his conversation with DirtFans.com, Gilbert recalled the party before the main event, and how some hair of the dog helped him to victory.

A week after winning the World 100, Floyd Gilbert captured the checkered flag of another major dirt race, the Johnny Appleseed Classic at Ohio's Mansfield Raceway. (John Nickelson photo, courtesy Eric Nickelson)

Floyd celebrates his win in the fourth annual Johnny Appleseed Classic at Mansfield, Ohio. The bowl-shaped trophy now resides in the National Dirt Late Model Hall of Fame. (John Nickelson photo, courtesy Eric Nickelson)

"Tiny Lund and I had been very drunk that night before... And I was so hung over; I never had a hangover like that before. So, the other four cars pass me and I'm running dead last, but at least I'm running. And the longer we go, and the heat, I got to feeling better and I ended up [fourth]," Gilbert recounted about the race's first segment. "So, I go up to the old bus and I drank two beers straight down. By the time I walked back down into the infield, I was feeling pretty good. I'd done come alive. They got the car ready to go, we lined up, and they threw that green flag. That beer must have had some kind of jet propulsion in it, because I was leading down the back straightaway."

Not exactly, but close. News accounts of the race show Gilbert started twelfth in the twenty-four-car field and advanced to fourth by the 75-lap midway break. After a short intermission, Gilbert needed just thirteen laps to roar from fourth to first to become the race's eighth and final leader. He was never challenged from there, holding off fellow Cincinnatian Bruce Merz as Ohio drivers took the top four spots. Gilbert also earned a $100 bonus for being the fastest qualifier.

Winning Continues in 1974

With no off-season changes except for a fresh coat of red paint on the Duncan Chevelle, the team's expectations were sky high. Predictably, victories arrived in bunches—mostly on dirt ovals dotting central Kentucky. The team's greatest success occurred during Friday night shows at Ponderosa Speedway, the banked 3/8-mile D-shaped track was the scene of eleven Gilbert victories in thirteen starts and the track championship. However, old favorite Glen Este soon stopped running stock cars and hosted only motorcycles, keeping Gilbert from seeking a fifth straight title close to home. And Clay City Raceway remained closed for a second straight year.

The season's first win came in the Ponderosa season opener April 26, and it was far from easy. Floyd started tenth but advanced to third in the race's first fourteen laps. It took four more circuits to get around Eddie Carrier for second place. Floyd then set sail for leader David Speer, who held Gilbert at bay for seventeen laps. Floyd finally slipped by, winning over Speer, Carrier, and Fats Coffey.

They won the 30-lap feature the following night at Whitewater Valley Speedway, with Gilbert, the fastest qualifier, forced to roll off from the eighth position. After working his way to the front, Floyd held off Gene Petro and Charlie Byrd for his second victory in about 24 hours.

On the Friday night preceding that year's Kentucky Derby, Ponderosa hosted a 50-lap Race of the Thoroughbreds that saw Gilbert lead the first 43 laps before fastest qualifier Billy Teegarden, piloting Morgan Chandler's Camaro, passed him for the eventual win. Floyd placed and Fats Coffey earned the show position, in horse racing parlance.

Gilbert then ripped off four consecutive Ponderosa victories. The streak began May 10, when he and Teegarden ran two laps door to door, scraping fenders before Floyd pulled ahead. Together they lapped the entire field. The win earned Floyd a spot on the cover of the May 17 *Mid-American Auto Racing News*.

The following night they resumed the battle at Bluestone Speedway as both Gilbert and Teegarden broke the track qualifying record before Tommy Day proved even quicker. Gilbert led the early laps but fell out with mechanical trouble. Teegarden took command until Sammy Robinson got on top of the guardrail on lap sixteen, bringing out the red flag. When rain began falling, the race was called complete.

Floyd returned to the Ponderosa winner's circle the following Friday, disposing of Ray Cash's Chevelle on lap eighteen. He led the remaining 22 circuits. Fastest qualifier Teegarden outran E.M. Snowden for second place.

His May 24 Memorial Weekend 50 Ponderosa victory required holding off E. M. Snowden Jr., who dogged the big red Duncan Chevelle for thirty straight laps before falling off the pace late in the going.

The following weekend, Gilbert captured a 25-lap feature at Ponderosa, posted a solid second behind Teegarden at Whitewater Valley, and then collected a $1,000 payday for winning over a star-packed field at Eldora Speedway on June 2, where Floyd outran Jim Patrick, Teegarden, Dick DeBolt, and Gene Petro. Fast qualifier Charlie Swartz was never a factor.

NASCAR star and former Daytona 500 winner Dewayne "Tiny" Lund and Gilbert became friends and racing rivals during the early 1970s. (John Butler photo)

Floyd and Tiny Lund would reprise their budding rivalry during the Art Meade 101 at Clarke's Motor Speedway, a banked Michigan half-mile oval, in a race run Wednesday night, June 12, before the NASCAR Winston Cup race at Michigan International Speedway.

Lund and Gilbert, who was identified as being from Kentucky, were booked in by promoter Rick Clarke as part of a three-driver Southern Team. The third member? NASCAR star Cale Yarborough, who was the winningest Winston Cup driver that season in Junior Johnson's Chevrolets. The southern team of Yarborough, Lund, and Gilbert ultimately defeated Michigan stars Ed Howe, Tom Maier, and Bob Senneker.

A crowd of about 5,000 turned out to witness sixty cars trying to qualify for the 24-car field. Yarborough was to race Senneker's big block

Chevelle backup car, but experienced engine failure during practice. Cale borrowed a car and finished second to Lund in the North-South challenge race, but car owner Frank Lamp wouldn't surrender the seat for the 101-lap feature.

Flyin' Floyd leans against the Duncan Chevelle – which sported new paint and larger numbers for the 1974 season – prior to a race at Clarke's Motor Speedway in Michigan where he competed with NASCAR stars Tiny Lund and Cale Yarborough. (Ray Rogers photo, courtesy Nelson Wirenga and Bob Markos)

Lund dominated the main event, with Floyd finishing a strong second and Michigan car builder Ed Howe third. Gilbert admitted he "couldn't beat" Lund but received a nice mention in the *Lansing State Journal* newspaper: "Even Floyd Gilbert, generally acknowledged to be the best dirt driver in the business, couldn't hold him [Lund] off," according to writer Dave Mathews.

After the mid-week Michigan race, Gilbert was back at Ponderosa on Friday night where he sustained his only other loss there all season, falling to Fats Coffey's 1965 Chevelle.

Floyd then put together another winning streak at Northern Kentucky Speedway in Florence, where he racked up four consecutive feature victories starting with the Gene Crittenden Memorial on June 28. After making some quick repairs under caution, he marched through the entire field to earn the win over Ron Edwards and Danny Eichler.

He also then won Bluestone Speedway's Firecracker 50 on Sunday June 29. Floyd wheeled the Duncan Chevelle past a field that included fast qualifier E.M. Snowden Jr., Vern LeFevers, and Jon Osmon.

Northern's Firecracker 50 on July 6 offered an $800 payday, which Floyd was more than happy to collect. He took the top spot from Dick DeBolt on lap fifteen and led the field to the checkers with John Mugavin second. Fast qualifier Larry Moore was never a factor. "My pit crew Logan and Charles Grider had the car in top shape as usual, and things just worked out good for me tonight," Floyd told writer Jim Wills.

Floyd earned his third straight at Florence on July 13, holding off second-place Bubby James and third-place Ron Edwards.

A jubilant Floyd Gilbert (right) celebrates with Northern Kentucky Speedway flagman Johnny Walter, after one of several 1974 victories at the Florence oval. (Courtesy Bob Markos, National Dirt Late Model Hall of Fame)

On July 20, Floyd withstood a late charge from an old rival, former USAC stock car rookie of the year Chuck McWilliams, in front of what promoters touted as the "largest crowd" in track history.

As part of concurrent winning streaks at Florence and Ponderosa, Floyd also nailed down Ponderosa's 100-lap Mid-Season Championship against a star-studded field of sixty cars from four states. He set fast time at 16.70 seconds and started from the pole, which was bad news for the field. Floyd put everyone except second-place David Speer a lap down. Despite a flat tire with two laps remaining, Speer held on for second, with E.M. Snowden Jr. finishing third.

Floyd didn't fare quite so well in another Clarke promotion at his old stomping grounds the Tri-County Speedway, which had been paved. On July 30, Gilbert and Chuck McWilliams were invited to race against some of the Midwest's finest pavement pilots in the 100-lap Challenge 1974 race, which also included Cale Yarborough.

Cale returned to the saddle of Senneker's Chevelle, won both North-South heat races, and advanced to fourth in the feature before the engine overheated. A crowd of 5.000 saw Senneker qualify on the pole, lead every lap, and collect the checkers in his lightweight, small-block Camaro. Fellow pavement stars John Anderson, Lennie Waldo, and Butch Miller finished second through fourth.

Gilbert and McWilliams "turned in creditable performances with their big-inch dirt cars but were overshadowed by the prowess of drivers who race on asphalt every week," reporter Terry Flynn wrote in the *Cincinnati Enquirer*. Floyd had predicted he might struggle a few days before, telling Flynn, "I think they might make a fool out of me. Of course, I made a fool out of them in Michigan, so I guess that's only fair."

Gilbert nabbed another $1,000 payday August 3 by earning the checkers in the Coca-Cola Invitational at Southern Ohio Raceway in Portsmouth. In another dominant run, Floyd took the lead from fastest qualifier Ron Edwards on the opening lap and led the entire sixty-lap feature on the high-banked half-mile dirt oval. Edwards ran a competitive second, while Pat Patrick finished third.

Sandwiched in that summer were two convincing 50-lap victories at

Kentucky's Bluestone Speedway. The first occurred July 21 in the Late Model Invitational. After early leaders E.M. Snowden and Billy Teegarden encountered mechanical troubles, Floyd held on to take the win, with Tommy Day second and Teegarden rebounding to run third.

Floyd Gilbert smiles after clinching the 100-lap Season Championship race at Ponderosa Speedway, his eleventh win in thirteen starts there in 1974. He is joined by sponsor E.C. Sheely. (Raymond Kelley photo, courtesy Fremont Speedway Hall of Fame, Mid-American Auto Racing News Archives)

He also captured Bluestone's Mid-Season Championship race August 10 by grabbing the lead on lap ten and outrunning Ray Cash, Teegarden, and Ned Lucas to the checkered flag. That last win came less than 24 hours after he again thumped the Friday night field at Ponderosa.

Floyd wrapped up the Ponderosa campaign on September 20, winning the 100-lap Season Championship race—his eleventh victory in thirteen starts—to claim the 1974 track title.

Back at Eldora Speedway in Ohio for the fifth annual World 100, Floyd's clean-shaven face appeared on the tickets and the program cover as the defending race champion. But October 13 proved unlucky for

Gilbert and the Duncan's Delight Chevelle. Pat Patrick set fast time, but with the invert, Floyd played his cards right and started on the front row. He picked up right where he left off—leading the sport's biggest race. Floyd paced the first 39 laps, with 1972 champion Verlin Eaker and Larry Moore in pursuit.

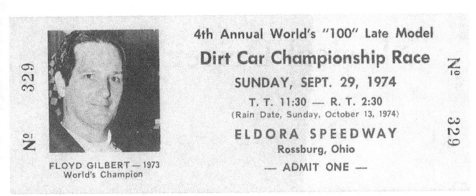

4th Annual World's "100" Late Model
Dirt Car Championship Race
SUNDAY, SEPT. 29, 1974
T. T. 11:30 — R. T. 2:30
(Rain Date, Sunday, October 13, 1974)

ELDORA SPEEDWAY
Rossburg, Ohio

— ADMIT ONE —

№ 329

FLOYD GILBERT — 1973
World's Champion

Tickets to the 1974 World 100 carried the image of defending champion Floyd Gilbert, who led the first 39 laps before being sidelined with a blown engine. (Courtesy Bob Markos, National Dirt Late Model Hall of Fame)

However, the engine under Floyd's hood blew as he entered turn one, sending the Chevelle into the outer guardrail and collecting Eaker. Jim Patrick inherited the top spot and led until his engine also failed, on lap 72. Iowan Ed Sanger was in the right place and held on to win over Ohioans Don Seaborn and Neal Sceva. Much like the previous year, only Sanger and Seaborn finished on the lead lap, with Seaborn trailing by a couple seconds at the stripe. Gilbert registered a fourteenth-place finish.

How challenging was the World 100, even in its infancy? It would be eleven seasons before Larry Moore became the first repeat World 100 winner, and it would take three more years before Jeff Purvis became the first driver to win in back-to-back seasons.

CHAPTER 11:

Musical Driver's Seats

Through the first half of the 1975 season, Gilbert drove—not for the Duncan team—but a pair of red, white, and blue Chevrolets fielded by HALS Racing, a group that included Kay Halland, Jim Abbott, Bob Larrick, and Richard "Jake" Skinner, from Winchester, Ohio. With Paul Hawlett's engine under the hood and crew member Larry Elrod keeping the cars on track, Floyd wheeled their Ed Howe-built Camaro to back-to-back early victories at Ohio's Brown County Speedway. They won the season opener April 13 over Baldy McLaren and Bobby Oney, then topped Calvin Kenneda and Ron Baker on April 20. Following a couple of strong second-place June finishes at Eldora Speedway, Floyd captured two straight victories at Earl Baltes' famed Ohio oval, at least one coming in the team's venerable 1968 Chevelle that carried Ray Cash to a dozen wins in 1974.

Further south in Kentucky, Gilbert ran a solid second to E.M. Snowden Jr., on May 9 at Ponderosa Speedway as Snowden debuted a gleaming new No. 59 1972 Chevelle out of the R.L. Duncan stable. Fats Coffey drove his new No. 10 Camaro to third place and Butterball Wooldridge finished fourth. Gilbert won his heat race the following Friday, but was never a factor in the Ponderosa feature, as Coffey's new Camaro outran Snowden.

Snowden won again in the Duncan Chevelle in Ponderosa's Memorial Day 50-lap feature on May 29, with Coffey second and Billy Childers third. Floyd repeated his heat race win, but didn't contend in the feature.

Gilbert began the 1975 season wheeling a No. 12 Camaro for the PALS Racing team. Together they won several feature races. Here Gilbert takes the high lane around Wilce LeFevers (No. 90) at Northern Kentucky Speedway. (Courtesy Fremont Speedway Hall of Fame, Mid-American Auto Racing News Archives)

On a return trip to Michigan, Gilbert was again labeled by the promoter as a Kentuckian and was among the featured drivers at the midweek Art Meade 101 run June 11 at Clarke's Motor Speedway. That put Gilbert on the South team, which also included NASCAR superstars Benny Parsons, David Pearson, and Cale Yarborough to race against a North team that included Danny Byrd, Ed Howe, Joe Ruttman, and Dick Trickle. But four of the eight didn't show up, and only the cars of Gilbert and Trickle were running at the end of the 101-lap feature.

The track was wet and muddy because a steady rain was falling when the green flag flew, according to a story in the *Lansing State Journal* newspaper. Yarborough and Pearson fell out and much of the contest was hampered by yellow flags that some leaders used to stop and remove mud from...well, everything. But unbeknownst to them, the caution laps counted—putting several challengers multiple laps down.

"Gilbert drove brilliantly, running away and hiding for 42 laps only to have a flat tire send him to the pits," *State Journal* writer Dave Mathews reported. Chicago-area star Jim O'Connor was declared the winner in a controversial finish, but runner-up Jim Nagy claimed he was leading in the muddy mess. It was days later before promoters finally awarded the win to Nagy, according to racing historian Bob Markos.

Closer to home at Northern Kentucky Speedway, Gilbert won often and seemingly could finish no worse than third. Northern changed its rules for the 1975 season, limiting late models to a single four-barrel carburetor and eleven-inch-wide tires. Despite some complaints about a rough racing surface, the half-mile oval regularly attracted many of the region's biggest names.

Floyd chased Billy Teegarden to the checkered flag in a 50-lap June 7 feature as Vern LeFevers was third and Pat Patrick fourth. On June 14, Floyd swept the dash, heat, and feature at NKS in the No. 12 Camaro, passing early leader Vern LeFevers with five laps remaining and outrunning LeFevers, Gene Petro, and fastest qualifier Pat Patrick.

Four nights later, Floyd posted a strong second-place behind Pat Patrick in the 60-lap Woody Fisher Stroh's feature. The two exchanged the lead, with Gilbert pacing laps four through 26 before Patrick pinned him behind some lapped traffic and held on for the $1,000 win. Floyd finished second ahead of Billy Teegarden, Bubby James, and Tom Helfrich. In the Saturday night NKS show, race leader Bubby James washed up high in turn four on lap 23, opening the door for Gilbert, who snagged the checkers over John Mugavin and Gene Petro.

E.M. Snowden's last win in the Duncan Chevelle occurred June 20 at Ponderosa, where he fended off Gene Petro. Gilbert replaced him the following Friday. The new car was a low-slung 1972 model, with a black vinyl top and exhausts exiting just ahead of the rear tires. The paint scheme was dark red metalflake with a hint of silver; anyone who saw the car with Flyin' Floyd behind the wheel immediately flashed back to 1972 and his 42-win season in Morgan Chandler's similarly styled vinyl top Chevelle. The impression was enhanced every time he went to victory lane, which was often.

Floyd encountered mechanical troubles in his debut effort June 27 in Ponderosa's 100-lap Mid-Season Championship race, a contest won by Gene Petro, with Fats Coffey second and Butterball Wooldridge third. Floyd bounced back to lead the June 28 feature at Northern Kentucky before breaking one of the new car's rear axles.

Floyd Gilbert worked out a unique beer sponsorship deal for this Chevelle, receiving 10 cases of beer a month in exchange for displaying Old Milwaukee on the quarter panels and hood. (Courtesy Fremont Speedway Hall of Fame, Mid-American Auto Racing News Archives)

Driving his own No. 1 Valley Radiator/Old Milwaukee Chevelle, Floyd earned two straight second-place finishes at Eldora before finally breaking through for a victory on June 29. Winning meant surviving a 10-lap duel with Vern LeFevers, who was coming off a winning the previous night at Florence. On lap 22, Floyd pinned Vern's green No. 13 Camaro behind a slower car to take the lead for good. LeFevers tagged the wall the next lap because the car's tie rod broke. Chick Hale ran second in Hoot Gibson's Camaro, and Russ Petro finished third. Fast qualifier Larry Moore experienced mechanical trouble and wasn't a factor.

Back in Kentucky, Gilbert set fast time of 15.80 seconds at Ponderosa July 4 but ran third in the feature behind Butterball Wooldridge and Gene Petro.

On July 23, 1975, Gilbert wheeled a new Duncan's Delight Chevelle to a $1,000 mid-week victory at Northern Kentucky Speedway. (John Butler photo, courtesy Fremont Speedway Hall of Fame, Mid-American Auto Racing News Archives)

Floyd guided the Duncan Chevelle to his third victory of the season at NKS July 5 and went on to capture two straight Wednesday night special shows there, including a July 23 beatdown when fastest qualifier Gene Petro led the first three laps, and Gilbert led the rest to earn a $1,000 payday. Petro trailed by three car-lengths at the finish, followed by Billy Teegarden, Vern LeFevers, and John Mugavin.

It was about that time the August issue of *Stock Car Racing* magazine appeared on newsstands—the issue carrying Carroll Hamilton's profile of Floyd, entitled "Fightin' Floyd Gilbert, Inc." Gilbert's name appeared on the cover and the story filled pages 54 and 55 before jumping to the back of the magazine.

"They say that the good old days of stock car racing are gone...the drinkin', fightin' carryin' on, an' all that," Hamilton wrote. "But there are still a few racers from the mold who sneak by into modern times. Some of them have become institutions."

Stock Car Racing Magazine's August 1975 issue carried a feature story about Floyd Gilbert written by Carroll Hamilton which dubbed Gilbert "master of the dirt." (Courtesy Drew Hierwarter)

The writer characterized Gilbert as a "holdover from days gone by," but a study in contrasts since he bridged the decades where the "roughest, toughest man won" to one who "mastered the art of muscling" race cars, while understanding the nuances of tuning and tire compounds.

The story was illustrated with John Butler photographs: one of Floyd clutching the iconic 1973 World 100 trophy in his left hand and a cup of beer in the right, the other an action shot of Morgan Chandler's virtually unbeatable 1972 Chevelle.

Just in time for his newfound fame, old stomping grounds Clay City Raceway reopened after being shuttered for two seasons. New promoters Dale Napper, Ronnie Roundtree, and Jim Swafford welcomed 35 late models on the opening Friday night. Pat Patrick set fastest time at 22.63 seconds aboard Morgan Chandler's Camaro and won the fast

Gilbert and the Duncan team collected several 1975 wins at Clay City Raceway in Kentucky, including the $1,000 Mid-Season Championship. (Ernest Thomas photo, courtesy author's collection)

heat, while Floyd captured the fast car dash. Patrick and Gerald Dixon exchanged the lead on the feature's first lap, but Gilbert and the Duncan Chevelle soon took command and led the remaining 29 circuits. Patrick finished right on his bumper in second while Jim Patrick got around Gerald Dixon for third and Jon Osman came home fifth.

Back at Clay City on July 25, and fresh off the aforementioned Wednesday night win at Northern Kentucky, Floyd again won the fast car dash but suffered mechanical trouble in his heat race. He was sidelined for the feature as fastest qualifier Billy Teegarden drove Earl Rogers' Camaro to the win, over Butterball Wooldridge and Ned Lucas.

The following night, Floyd won his heat race at Florence but finished second in the main event to Chuck McWilliams, who notched his first victory of the year. Vern LeFevers finished third.

Floyd ran third behind Pat Patrick and West Virginia ace Larry Brumfield in Clay City's August 1 feature, driving a different 1968 model Duncan vinyl top Chevelle. The following week, Floyd tangled with Brumfield and his No. 511 Camaro.

On August 8 at Clay City, Butterball Wooldridge grabbed the early lead, but Gilbert powered the Duncan Chevelle by him on lap three. Two circuits later, Gilbert and Larry Brumfield got together on the backstretch while racing for the top spot, with Gilbert's Chevelle exiting over the turn three banking. Brumfield led the next fourteen laps before 24-year-old Tom Helfrich took the lead and never looked back. Wooldridge finished second in a No. 77 Camaro owned by Jack Wagner and built by Ray Callahan. Gilbert, after re-starting at the rear of the nineteen-car field, soldiered back to finish third.

Looking back on that time, Helfrich said his weekly four-hour treks to Clay City provided great learning experiences.

"We went to Clay City and Northern Kentucky to learn from two of the best at that time in Floyd Gilbert and Pat Patrick. Then you throw Billy Teegarden in there too," Helfrich said in a 2018 interview. "They were very fierce competitors, they drove very up-to-date cars, and they were what you wanted to be if you wanted to learn anything or hone your skills.

"I became friends with Morgan Chandler when Pat Patrick drove for him, and Logan Grider and his brother when Floyd Gilbert drove for them. We'd stay overnight, and if we had work to do, we'd go to Morgan Chandler's shop. And you know everybody pretty much was building their own cars back then. It wasn't cookie cutter like today," Helfrich said.

But Helfrich soon learned a valuable lesson racing with Gilbert: don't poke the bear.

"One night at Northern [Kentucky], I was still trying to learn how to drive. I gave Floyd Gilbert a little bit of a run. I got into his back bumper a little bit. Well, he marched right down there—I'll never forget this—he kind of set me straight, then he grinned a little bit when he left," Helfrich recalled. "I remember Logan [Grider] came over and was tickled to death to see me run like that. There was some rubbing and some really hard racing. Cars were built a little different back then."

Floyd was first and fastest August 2 at Northern Kentucky, setting quick time, winning the dash and the feature aboard the Duncan Chevelle. Long-time rivals Pat Patrick and Gene Petro finished second and third, respectively.

The following Saturday, Gilbert finished third in a three-car train at Northern Kentucky as Vern LeFevers took the top spot and Tom Helfrich finished second in the 100-lap Mid-Season Championship.

Thursday nights that summer featured the Kentucky Dirt Track Racing Association's National Dirt Track championship series: five races at five central Kentucky ovals. The series held its fourth stop at Northern Kentucky August 7. In the 50-lap feature, Floyd passed fast qualifier Ron Edwards after an early caution and led to the checkers. Edwards ran a solid second, followed by Gene Petro and William "Fats" Coffey.

Coffey won the fifth and final race August 21 at Ponderosa Speedway to claim the championship over Butterball Wooldridge, who also recorded two wins. Coffey held off Gerald Dixon, Gilbert, and Eddie Carrier in Bobby Paul's Camaro, and Wooldridge at the checkers. Gilbert wound up sixth in the series points.

That summer also brought a somber reminder about the dangers of racing, as Gilbert's friend Tiny Lund was killed in a racing accident August 17 in a NASCAR Grand National race at Talladega, Alabama.

Pat Patrick and Gilbert raced hard for thirty laps before finishing first and second respectively at Clay City on August 22. Patrick turned the hat trick by setting fast time, then winning the dash, heat, and feature. Patrick was also the class of the field the following night at Northern, leading all 100 laps of the Kentucky Dirt Track feature, as Chuck McWilliams ran second in a race where Tom Helfrich suffered a major crash in his Camaro.

Next up was the August 29 Mid-Season Championship race, a 50-lap feature at Clay City offering a $1,000 winner's payday. Fast qualifier Pat Patrick started out front and led the first twenty-two circuits before Gilbert thundered by, lapping the entire field by the time the checkered flag flew. Larry Brumfield finished second, Pat Patrick third, Fred Dillow came home fourth, and Ned Lucas rounded out the top five.

It was Patrick's turn to win August 30 at Northern, holding off Ron Edwards and Gene Petro on a night when Rick Shepherd's No. 91 Chevelle—a car formerly raced by Gilbert—got up on the guardrail and embedded the car nose first, standing it straight up in the air. A shaken Shepherd walked away.

Gilbert visited Frankfort Speedway August 31 and won the Season Championship race after a thrilling duel with Gene Petro. Top qualifier Butterball Wooldridge, driving the Jack Wagner No. 77 Camaro, led the first fifteen circuits before giving way to Petro in the Ruth Motors Nova. He led 28 circuits of the 75-lap feature before Gilbert pinned Petro behind a slower car, dove to the bottom, and successfully made the pass. Floyd held on for a $600 victory over Petro, Wooldridge, Fats Coffey, and Tommy Day.

Patrick and Gilbert were again the class of the Clay City field on September 12. Fast timer Patrick drew a tenth-place starting position, forcing him to share the fifth row in the 21-car field with Gilbert, who had qualified second. Patrick grabbed the lead after a lap three restart, while Gilbert spun but was able to work back to the second spot by the end of the 30-lap feature. Butterball Wooldridge, Billy Teegarden, and Charlie Perry completed the top five.

Despite another superb season, Floyd also wound up second to Patrick in the points standings at Northern Kentucky, as Patrick powered the Morgan Chandler Camaro to three wins in late August and early September to sew up the title. Patrick only had to qualify at the season championship race. He did more than that, finishing a car-length behind race winner and fast qualifier Gene Petro.

Floyd's third World 100 driving for the Duncan team was far less successful than the first two, because the 1973 winner and 1974 race leader was never a factor in 1975. With a field of 168 of the country's best late models assembled at Eldora on September 21, Gilbert started twelfth in the elite 22-car field. Gilbert had timed in twelfth fastest in qualifying, with a lap of 20.369 seconds: a half-second off the pace of top qualifier Billy Teegarden in the Ruben Brothers No. 22 Camaro, at 19.870.

However, mechanical problems before the race's halfway point relegated the big red Chevelle to a poor twentieth-place finish and a meager $100 payday. After starting tenth, Iowa's Joe Merryfield wheeled his Chevelle to a convincing $8,000 victory over defending champion Ed Sanger, Verlin Eaker, Danny Eichler, and Dave Yobe. Georgian Doug Kenimer led the middle segment of the race but faded to finish tenth.

Mechanical problems again reared their ugly head the following weekend at an even richer race, costing Gilbert a shot at winning $10,000. The World Dirt Championship Cavalcade of Champions was a landmark event in dirt racing history that September 27-28, and Gilbert was in the thick of the action for much of the day. He timed the Duncan Chevelle in fifth quickest behind Iowa hitters Ed Sanger and Ken Walton, World 100 champ Joe Merryfield, and Wisconsin's Tom Steuding. Floyd missed the pole by just over a quarter-second around the Ionia, Michigan Fairgrounds. For good measure, Floyd brought his own Chevelle and qualified 37th of the ninety cars that filled the pit area.

"Floyd got up to second behind Tom Steuding, until Doug Kenimer passed both him and Steuding," racing historian Bob Markos recalled. "Steuding dropped out, and Floyd was the only guy who could stay with Kenimer. He stayed with him until lap seventy-five, when the Duncan Chevelle came to the pits with a broken fuel pump. From there Kenimer checked out."

The Georgia ace—relying on Ernie Elliott horsepower—held off Merryfield, who collected $5,000 for second place; Ed Sanger ran third.

The disappointment of losing those two marquee races led to Gilbert leaving a team in which he had "made a good living."

"I start outside pole, and one of these guys that has since won the World 100 was inside. He took the lead, and I'm running second. I'm happy—hell, I'm running second; that pays $5000," Gilbert told DirtFans. com. "That's when the fuel pump broke off the block. Just broke off. And I pulled it in and I didn't say nothing. Anyway, I lost sixty-eight hundred dollars in breakdowns that year. That's when I just about decided I was going to quit Duncan."

Gilbert was a no-show for Clay City's 50-lap Season Championship contest October 5 on a day Pat Patrick led every lap. Patrick claimed the day's $1,000 top prize over runner-up Tom Helfrich, Tye Long, Delmas Conley, and Wooldridge, who had temporarily returned to the Duncan Chevelle. The win enabled Patrick to edge out Gilbert for the Clay City track championship.

CHAPTER 12:

Old Big Iron

Floyd Gilbert drove at least five different cars for three different owners during the 1975 season, including a handful of starts in the Camaro of Cincinnati-based team owner Earl Rogers, sponsored by Ruben Brothers Auto Parts. The combination had fielded winning race cars for many years, including for Gene Cleveland and Billy Teegarden. For the 1976 campaign, they were more than happy to letter *Floyd* on the doors of their blue, white, and red Camaro, powered by engines affectionately dubbed "Old Big Iron."

The landscape was shifting and top-quality rides were hard to land. While Pat Patrick didn't win 42 features, his two track championships and regular wins kept him solidly in the saddle of Morgan Chandler's Camaro. Butterball reunited with the Duncan bunch to wheel their 1968 Chevelle, Billy Teegarden started the year with Larry Morrison, and Gene Petro stayed with the Ruth Motors team, which debuted a brand-new Camaro. Kentucky car owner Bobby Paul hired David Speer and Finn Watson for a potent two-car team, while stalwarts like Fats Coffey and Tom Helfrich again fielded their own cars.

Gilbert continued to score big payday wins at rugged Northern Kentucky but emerged winless in just eight starts driving four different cars at favorite stomping grounds Clay City. Victories also came at Eldora, Ponderosa, and Brown County Speedway in Ohio.

But the checkered flags were becoming more elusive, and the cars were rapidly evolving. The steel Chevelles with torquey big-block engines that had dominated the scene for so many years were being replaced by lighter Camaros with tubular chassis, and many relied on lighter, higher winding small-block engines.

The Earl Rogers Camaro still relied on big-block Chevy power, and had been the top qualifier at the 1975 World 100, with Billy Teegarden setting fast time. As Floyd told DirtFans.com, the team worked hard and had fun.

"After Duncan, I went with Earl Rogers in the Ruben Brothers' number twenty-two. It wasn't no mistake, in other words financially, it was a mistake," Floyd said. "But as far as the guys, I enjoyed them. They were a lot of fun, and they had a lot of beer. They kept that Blue Ribbon in the refrigerator all the time. I would go down there about every night when they were working on the car. And I would drink their beer. That was my rights; I had beer rights."

Floyd assembled two early victories at Northern Kentucky, including a May 8 battle with young Bubby James, who started on the pole and led the first fifteen laps. Gilbert got around James on the frontstretch, but he battled back in turn one only to see Gilbert maintain control. Fast qualifier Tom Helfrich pressured Gilbert on a late restart, but Floyd held on for the win with Helfrich, James, Gene Petro, and Chuck McWilliams rounding out the top five. Floyd also won the fast heat.

Gilbert again sparred with Helfrich the following weekend to claim the $1,000 top prize in a 30-lap feature at Eldora Speedway. This time, Helfrich led the first 24 circuits before Gilbert got around him for the win. Helfrich finished second and Delmas Conley was third, while fast qualifier Billy Teegarden and Bubby James rounded out the top five. Things got a bit easier two weeks later when Floyd led all 25 laps, holding off Petro and Teegarden to earn his second Northern Kentucky victory of the month.

The performance gap was more apparent May 21 at Clay City, where Gilbert ran third in the fast dash, third in the fast heat, and fourth in the feature, getting no higher than third and finishing behind Butterball Wooldridge, Pat Patrick, and E.M. Snowden Jr.

For 1976, Floyd primarily drove for car owner Earl Rogers and his No. 22 Camaro. "Ole Big Iron," carried Gilbert to the 1976 Northern Kentucky Speedway points championship. (Courtesy Fremont Speedway Hall of Fame, Mid-American Auto Racing News Archives)

Floyd earned a Northern Kentucky sweep June 14, winning the dash, heat, and feature, but only after dogging Vern LeFevers Camaro for the first twenty laps of the main event. Floyd slipped by and led the final five circuits with Vern second, followed by Gene Petro, top qualifier Pat Patrick, and Billy Teegarden.

Floyd returned to victory lane at Northern Kentucky June 21 on a night when the engine under his hood was as warm as rival Gene Petro. Gilbert was fast qualifier and won the fast car dash, but trailed Petro's Ruth Motors Camaro late in the 25-lap feature. Petro's car got out of shape and following a tap from Gilbert's front bumper, spun on the backstretch. According to *OKI Racing News*, the pack "parted like the Red Sea" to avoid Petro's white and red Chevy—except for Tommy Day, who tagged Petro virtually head-on.

After the red flag was lifted, Floyd led the restart and held on for the win over Bubby James, Pat Patrick, and Chuck McWilliams, who exhibited steam spewing from beneath his hood.

A week later, Floyd won the fast car dash but ran fourth in a feature won by Billy Teegarden. On June 27, Gilbert and Gene Petro traded the Eldora fast heat race lead six times before Floyd snagged the win. Their battle continued in the feature; Floyd led early before being passed by eventual winner Petro. He ultimately lost the runner-up spot to Billy Teegarden and finished third.

In Northern Kentucky's 76-lap July 3 Bicentennial race, Floyd offered a stiff mid-race challenge against leader Teegarden, but couldn't surpass the Duncan Chevelle. Gilbert wound up in second place, with points rival Pat Patrick finishing third.

Floyd set fast time the following Friday at Ponderosa Speedway but was sidelined early by engine trouble while challenging eventual winner Gene Petro for the lead. The following night, Floyd battled Petro for the victory at Northern Kentucky, as Petro went two for two.

Gilbert earned one of his more eventful victories July 11 at Ohio's Brown County Speedway, wheeling the No. 12 HALS Racing Camaro to win a race cut short by a red flag after two run-ins with Bubby James. James was leading the scheduled 20-lap feature, with Gilbert applying pressure. Gilbert tapped James' rear bumper and brushed his door as he passed on the inside. As reported in *Mid-American Auto Racing News*, "James went after Gilbert down the backstretch and drove into him in the number three turn. James got the worst end of the encounter; James spun over the bank and the yellow flag came out."

James then re-entered the track and was black flagged but remained on track and drove into Gilbert again in turns three and four. Floyd kept his car going in the right direction, while James again sailed over the turn three embankment. At that moment, the red flag was displayed and the race was called complete at lap 19. That, however, was not the end of the story; James and the track owner reportedly exchanged words, and Bubby was ultimately barred from future races.

"Gilbert pulled up to the finish line, took the checkered flag, and was ready to get his picture taken by track photographer Stan Jeffrey," according to the published account. "At that instant, one of the people with James' car threw an egg intended for Gilbert and hit Jeffrey's camera and shirt."

It's worth noting the previous night at Northern, Bubby got the worst of a tough three-way battle for fifth place and that contact shuffled him out of contention for the night.

On July 17, Floyd was the fastest qualifier at 19.38 seconds and led the first 41 laps of Northern Kentucky's Mid-Season Championship race before Pat Patrick slipped by. Patrick went on to post the win in the Chandler Camaro, while Gilbert faded to fourth behind Gene Petro and John Mugavin.

After qualifying seventh, Floyd ran as high as fourth before being sidelined by blown head gasket at Clay City's July 23 Mid-Season Championship. Jim Patrick won that race and the $1,500 top prize in Dave Bailey's Camaro, with Billy Teegarden second. Floyd won a heat race the following night at Florence but finished eighth in the feature, which went to John Mugavin.

Floyd resumed winning at Brown County Speedway July 25, setting fast time and sweeping the fast dash, fast heat, and feature over Ed Eschmann, Bob Prather and Matt Gilardi.

Gilbert finished fourth behind winner Fats Coffey, Ricky Spalding, and Finn Watson in a 76-lap feature July 30 at Ponderosa. He bounced back to win the next night at Northern Kentucky, outrunning Dick DeBolt and Gene Petro to the checkers.

On August 6, Gilbert drove the Bailey Brothers Rechrome No. 37 Camaro to a hard-fought runner-up finish in the 50-lap Clay City Invitational. After starting third, Gilbert stayed glued to race leader Pat Patrick's rear bumper all night as the lead pair lapped the entire field. Gilbert finished second ahead of Butterball Wooldridge, who was again driving for the Duncan team.

The following night at Florence, Gilbert steered the No. 37 to victory in the fast dash but settled for a fourth-place feature finish behind Gene Petro, Bubby James, and John Mugavin.

Floyd returned to the No. 22 Camaro the following Friday at Clay City, starting fourth and finishing fifth behind Pat Patrick (who had started on the tail of the 19-car field), Tom Helfrich, Tudy Adkins, and Ned Lucas. The next night at Florence, Gilbert qualified second behind John Mugavin's Firebird and ran third in the fast dash. However, the program was cut short after an amateur class car spun into a backstretch pit entrance where many people were standing, sending thirteen to the hospital.

A week later at Clay City, Floyd subbed for Ned Lucas in the Addington Bros. Mining No. 7 Camaro and started on the pole. He finished third behind Teegarden, who won in the Duncan Chevelle, and fastest qualifier Tom Helfrich. Among other changes, Butterball Wooldridge was in the Bruce Back Bluegrass Auto No. 4 Camaro, formerly driven by Billy Childers.

On August 27, more than 55 cars filled the Clay City pits to overflowing for the Labor Day 100 and its $1,500 top prize. Gilbert made a single start for car owner Morgan Chandler, while Pat Patrick qualified both the Bruce Merz No. 1 Motor Specialists Camaro and the No. 5 Camaro and won the fast dash. Charlie Swartz returned to the controls of Dave Bailey's No. 37 Camaro and was the fastest qualifier, at 22.70 seconds.

Fog descended on the Clay City track as the 20-car feature field was being lined up. Swartz passed early leader Tom Helfrich on lap five and led until a Gerald Dixon spin brought out the race's first caution on lap sixteen. The next five laps were run under caution due to the worsening visibility; the race was eventually called at lap 23, with Floyd running fourth.

Rather than restart at that point two weeks later, promoters decided to run the full 100 laps on September 5. Billy Teegarden survived a spirited battle by passing Swartz with five laps to go, claiming a $1,500 payday. Delmas Conley was third, with E.M. Snowden Jr. fourth; Gilbert finished fifth, driving the Ned Lucas No. 7 Camaro.

While Floyd struggled to win on Friday nights at Clay City, he finished first, second, and fourth, plus earned a pole, in three August races at Northern Kentucky. With one race was cancelled, and another at month's end was rained out, Gilbert led Northern's late model standings by more than 140 points over second-place Pat Patrick and third-place Gene Petro.

At season's end, Gilbert finally clinched his long-sought Northern

Kentucky track points championship and claimed season honors at the Brown County oval.

Floyd entered the U.S. Dirt Track Championships at Champagne, Illinois, in September but fell short of race winner Charlie Hughes, second-place Doug Kenimer, and third-place Jim O'Connor.

Gilbert nearly won Clay City's 1976 season finale, which attracted the usual crowd from Cincinnati and central Kentucky, plus western Kentucky stars Jesse Ladd and Jerry Rhoades. Floyd qualified fifth quickest in the No. 37. Camaro, then won the fast car dash and finished second in the fast heat.

Floyd led the first fifteen laps of the abbreviated 20-lap feature before the car suffered a broken shock mount. Pat Patrick, driving the No. 1 Motor Specialists Camaro, slipped past with laps winding down to claim the win and relegate Gilbert to second. E.M. Snowden Jr. finished third after starting eleventh, while Eddie Carrier and Ned Lucas rounded out the top five.

The following week Floyd posted his best World 100 finish since the 1973 victory, scoring a strong fourth-place run despite being involved in the race's first caution. Gilbert tangled with fastest qualifier Delmas Conley on the frontstretch, but both veterans were able to continue.

Floyd worked his way up to second place by lap five and held that position until Georgia ace Charlie Hughes used an inside move off turn four to get by him on lap sixteen. Helfrich slipped past Gilbert three laps later; Hughes—who had started tenth—took the lead that same lap. Fellow Georgian Doug Kenimer was also sailing through the pack. He wrestled fourth place from Gilbert on lap 26, and then passed both Helfrich and Sanger for second on lap 33.

Gilbert mounted a late charge to pass Sanger but was unable to catch Helfrich for third. Hughes won, holding off Kenimer in their lightweight small-block Camaros. Helfrich finished third, followed by Gilbert, who took home $650. The top ten also included 1974 World 100 champion Ed Sanger. Billy Teegarden, Gene Petro, and John Mugavin, who finished sixth, seventh, and eighth respectively.

CHAPTER 13:

Racing & Winning Down South

Having spent the past few winters racing in Florida and Georgia to help pay the bills, Gilbert had an appreciation for the differences in race track surfaces and chassis setups from the Midwest to the much sandier soil found in and around Jacksonville and Daytona Beach.

At the end of the 1976 season, Floyd Gilbert—soon to be 47 years old—made a critical career decision. However, he followed the lead of

Floyd was a pioneer in leading Midwestern drivers south in the winter to continue racing and pick up some extra money. Here Gilbert is pictured at a Florida track with his infamous homemade tow vehicle, dubbed the "ten ton turd." (Courtesy author's collection.)

longtime friend and rival Gene Petro and moved his racing operation to Florida. Rather than planning to return home each summer as Petro did, Floyd decided most the of the remainder of his career would play out in the deep south.

He spent part of the summer racing at his old haunts like Northern Kentucky and Whitewater, but the headlines typically belonged to his rivals.

However, Gilbert let everyone know he was back in the Midwest during an August 1977 interview with the *Cincinnati Enquirer* before a race at Northern Kentucky Speedway.

"Up until last year, we hadn't won enough down there hardly to buy steaks on the way home. Now we're the ones to beat," Floyd told reporter Tim Sullivan. In typical Flyin' Floyd style, he also used the moment to don the black hat.

"I don't need friends in racing. I want enemies," Gilbert said, doubtless smiling all the while. "You treat your friends differently on the track. With people you don't know, you don't care about bending their sheet

Gilbert returned home in the summer of 1977 to drive Earl Rogers No. 22 Camaro, here winning the Mid-Season Championship at Northern Kentucky. He qualified this car fourth quickest in the World 100 and finished top-ten. (Courtesy Fremont Speedway Hall of Fame, Mid-American Auto Racing News Archives)

metal or sending them into the wall."

During his venture back home, Floyd put together another solid top-ten finish at the 1977 World 100, again driving for Earl Rogers and the Ruben Brothers. He qualified fourth in the Camaro behind Georgia's Snooks DeFoor, Tennessean H.E. Vineyard, and Ohio's Rodney Combs. That locked him into the field, allowing Floyd to miss the annual heat race melee; more than 170 other hot shoes attempted to make the show.

With a record 10,000 fans looking on, sixth qualifier Tom Helfrich started on the pole, with Billy Thomas outside and Gilbert inside of row two. DeFoor rocketed into the top spot on lap one and led the first thirty laps. Doug Kenimer took the lead on the 31st circuit and paced the field to the checkers to collect the $10,000 payday. DeFoor finished second, followed by Helfrich, Ed Sanger, Ken Walton, Gilbert (who ran in the top six all day), Ronnie Faith, Billy Thomas, Billy Teegarden, Vern LeFevers, and former NASCAR Grand National regular Bill Morton.

Floyd ran the World 100 once more, in 1978, but was unable to contend for its $11.000 top prize. For the first time, Gilbert failed to lock himself into the show during qualifying, forcing him to battle through his heat race. He finished seventeenth in the main event, one spot ahead of old rival Bubby James. But other longtime rivals, including Pat Patrick, Billy Teegarden, and Rodney Combs—the fastest qualifier—all earned top-ten finishes.

Down south, much of Floyd's Florida success was due to a car built and painted in Ohio, one that followed Vern LeFevers' lead: sporting green paint and the number 13, both considered taboo at that time in most stock car racing circles.

"Somehow or another, John Holmes ended up with this Howe chassis. What he knew about a chassis I don't know, but it handled as good as any car I ever drove. But John gave me the car, and I worked on it for about a month. I figured I would take it with me to Florida. It was in the winter. So, in comes Vern," Floyd told DirtFans.com.

"What color are you going to paint it?" LeFevers asked.

"Hell, I don't know," Gilbert replied.

"How about green?" LeFevers asked—an interesting question, since

Vern once piloted a green Camaro owned by Jim Deitz.

"You go get the paint and we'll paint it green," Floyd said. "That saved me a gallon of paint. I didn't have much money back in the winter time. So, he went and got the paint, and we painted it green."

"What number you going to put on it?" LeFevers then asked.

"Hell, I don't know," Floyd replied.

"How about thirteen?" asked LeFevers, whose green Jim Deitz Camaro also wore that number.

"You go get the paint and put it on there," Floyd recalled.

"I brought it out to Florida, Pecan Park out here, and they said, 'You'll never make no money with this car.' They dumped beer in it, and peanut shells, and everything else. It took a while after I got rid of the four-fifty-four engines and went to the four twenty-seven until I really got it hooked up. There was nothing down there that handled like it. It felt good driving out in the fluff, passing."

Later in his career, Gilbert discovered that Cadillac engines from the junkyards came in 472 and 500 cubic-inch displacement, offering tons of torque and power on a budget, Floridian Mark Gibson recalled.

Ironically, something seemingly innocuous had impeded Floyd's success in his earliest ventures south—until he convinced promoters to change the rules.

"We weren't winning, and we had to run a windshield. I'm the one that got them to change to where we could run a screen instead of a windshield. They used oil on those old sand tracks to hold them together, and sometimes you couldn't see. They had a yellow [flag], you would unbuckle and get out, sit on the door and wipe the windshield," he told DirtFans.com. However, the change took a couple years.

"We carried a windshield with us and we carried a screen with us. until one day I went out with a screen and we ran. And the old man seemed to kinda like it. But I cut a hole in mine, cause the screen looked like fifteen screens to me. But it turned out, though, that that helped a hell of a lot, cutting the hole. It hurt me a couple times, though, because I got hit in the eye once. I guess I got hit in the eye twice," Gilbert said.

From Jacksonville and Pecan Park to East Bay and Oglethorpe Speedway in Savannah, Georgia, Floyd raced sometimes five nights a week, competing against other snowbirds like old friend Gene Petro, former NASCAR pavement standout Sam Sommers, Floridian Will Cagle, Georgia invader Doug Kenimer, and a host of others.

A sampling of results shows Gilbert ran third in the 1978 Southern Late Model Nationals at East Bay, behind John Berg and Ohioan Ron Leaser. He ran third again the following night, behind Kenimer and Cagle, after winning a heat race.

Gilbert finally hung up his helmet around 1980 as the wave of small-block cars strangled out his preferred big blocks.

"That happened up at Oglethorpe; they had one light car, small block, that run up there all the time. He was competitive, but I could usually beat him by the end of feature time," Gilbert said. "Knowledge I know of the small block is that you rebuild them and they're a very powerful motor, but every race you run them they get weaker. To the point you have to rebuild them again. In fact, I would say you would have to rebuild them every two or three months. My big block I rebuilt maybe once a year; I never had much trouble with motors."

CHAPTER 14:

Rivals & Friends

A tired sports cliché demands one must "beat the best to be the best." In the case of Flyin' Floyd Gilbert, racing side by side with and often beating multiple generations of dirt racing superstars defined his remarkable career. He was driven to succeed at a high level, with the mantra "I didn't come to run second." Had he practiced his craft somewhere else, against lesser competition, he might have scored 1,000 feature wins instead of the 500 he is credited with—but he was pushed at every turn.

From his earliest days on the track with Ralph and Bernie Latham to Chuck McWilliams, Rodney Combs, Larry Moore, Pat Patrick, Billy Teegarden, Butterball Wooldridge, and all the rest, Gilbert carved out his piece of history during the golden age of dirt late-model racing.

A hard-nosed racer who won regularly, Floyd Gilbert (right) had more rivals than friends. But one of his closest pals was fellow Hall of Famer Gene Petro. (Courtesy Paula Gilbert)

One example is Floyd's relationship with one of his closest rivals, Saylor Park's Pat Patrick.

"Pat was one of the better drivers that I was never afraid to be around in a race car. Pat knew dirt pretty well. Fact is, I had two cars, and I let Pat drive one for a while. I put Billy Teegarden in a car too and guaranteed him $100 a week. And I paid off on that a few times when it rained," he said.

Surprisingly, Gilbert believed Patrick may have given him a gift or two.

"I think Pat actually let me win a couple of races," he said. "One of them that comes to mind was at Whitewater Valley Speedway. He had this damn race locked up and coming in for the checker flag, I passed him. And I couldn't pass him ten laps before. Final ten laps I couldn't pass him... I really think he let me beat him that night. He didn't need the money. The guy that owned his car didn't need the money. I was battling for whatever I could get."

Among the world class drivers that Floyd shared the track with were:

Eddie Carrier Sr.

A native of Burgin, Ky., "Big Eddie" is known today as crew chief for his son, Eddie Carrier Jr. But he was a standout driver in the 1970s and 1980s, and a force to be reckoned with on bullrings like Ponderosa and Richmond, Kentucky. He was the first driver for team owner Bobby Paul, fielded his own cars, and later gained his greatest fame driving for team owner Bob Miller and the Miller Bros. Coal entry along with teammate H.E. Vineyard, at major races. Carrier was inducted into the National Dirt Hall of Fame in 2013.

William "Fats" Coffey

One of the most dominant drivers in Bluegrass state history, the Greensburg, Kentucky native was most successful on the tight Kentucky bullrings like Glasgow, Richmond, Taylor County, Ponderosa, Franklin County, and Barren County. His green No. 10 machines were always a factor, whether it was setting fast time or winning the feature. Coffey was inducted into the National Dirt Hall of Fame in 2015.

Delmas Conley

A trucking company owner from Wheelersburg, Ohio, Delmas Conley viewed racing as a hobby, a very serious hobby that he continued pursuing well into his 70s. Conley once dominated the action at Southern Ohio Raceway in Portsmouth, and competed at tracks all over Kentucky, Ohio, West Virginia, and Indiana, winning more than 500 feature races. He was inducted into the National Dirt Late Model Hall of Fame in 2003.

Rodney Combs

Nicknamed "The Rocket" early in his remarkable career, the Ohio native amassed more than 350 dirt feature race victories in two distinctly different decades. Combs broke into the late model winner ranks at the age of 20, scoring notable victories as early as 1970. He became a force in the National Dirt Racing Association, winning its 1983 championship, finishing points runner-up twice, and winning fifteen series races. Combs made more than 180 starts in NASCAR's top three divisions in the 1980s and 1990s driving for Richard Petty and J.D. Stacy, among others. He was inducted into the National Dirt Late Model Hall of Fame in 2001.

Jim Curry

With a career that included more than 400 victories across four decades, Indiana native Jim Curry was an institution over the late model stockers broad evolution from steel bodies and big blocks to purpose-built, small-block flyers. Beginning in 1970, Curry racked up big money wins across Indiana, Illinois, Kentucky, and Ohio. He was inducted into the National Dirt Late Model Hall of Fame in 2003.

Bruce Gould

One of the most decorated drivers to emerge from the Cincinnati short track wars, Bruce Gould was as proficient on pavement as dirt. He competed in ARCA, USAC, and NASCAR Grand National East during the 1970s, winning seventeen ARCA new car series feature races—including four combo races with the GN East stars. Gould was a force at Tri-County, Northern Kentucky, and Glen Este on a weekly basis, and captured the initial World 100 title in 1971. He returned to dirt after ARCA and continued to excel. He finished with more than 300 feature victories and was inducted into the National Dirt Late Model Hall of Fame in 2009.

Tom Helfrich

Branded the "Haubstadt Hustler," from his Indiana hometown, Helfrich amassed more than 300 feature race wins. Five of those were in the National Dirt Racing Association in the 1980s, including the 1984 Stroh's Invitational. He captured the USA World 50 at Paducah, Kentucky in 1980, and finished second in the World 100 in 1990. He was inducted into the National Dirt Late Model Hall of Fame's second class in 2002. At this writing, he and his wife Loris still operate Tri-State Speedway in Indiana.

Ralph Latham

Latham was a dominant force in Cincinnati area dirt track action in the 1960s. He went on to a successful career in ARCA and USAC, winning six ARCA new car series races, including the 1967 ARCA 200 at Daytona. He won several track championships and drove for many of the era's top car owners, such as Porter Lanigan, Luther McDonald, Morgan Chandler, and Jim Cook. He scored 400 feature wins and was inducted into the National Dirt Late Model Hall of Fame in 2006.

Vern LeFevers

One of the most prolific winners from the same era as Gilbert, LeFevers is credited with more than 650 feature race wins and nineteen track championships across Ohio, Kentucky, and Indiana. LeFevers is among the most recognized wheelmen from a career that began in the 1960s, and he drove for many of the era's top car owners. Once bitter rivals, LeFevers and Floyd eventually became friends. He was inducted into the National Dirt Late Model Hall of Fame in 2006.

Dubbed the "three amigos," Gene Petro, Vern LeFevers (center) and Floyd Gilbert were rivals and friends. (Courtesy Fremont Speedway Hall of Fame, Mid-American Auto Racing News Archives)

Chuck McWilliams

One of Floyd's toughest rivals, especially during the late 1960s, was Union Kentucky's Chuck McWilliams: winner of the 1968 and 1969 Tri-County Speedway championships, and a former champ at Northern Kentucky. McWilliams went on to earn USAC stock car division rookie of the year in 1972, the same year he won twice in that touring series. He also competed sparingly in the ARCA series. The winner of 300 feature races, McWilliams was inducted into the National Dirt Late Model Hall of Fame in 2008.

Chuck McWilliams raced with Floyd throughout the 1960s and 1970s and was one of his most fierce rivals. Here he is pictured winning a race in one of Morgan Chandler's cars. (Courtesy Fremont Speedway Hall of Fame, Mid-American Auto Racing News Archives)

John Mugavin

A former champion at Northern Kentucky Speedway and Glen Este Speedway, John Mugavin raced wheel to wheel with Gilbert and all the other stars of the 1960s and 1970s, claiming his share of victories. Like so many in the era, Mugavin built his own cars and raced out of his auto body shop in Ohio. Unofficially, Mugavin won more than 200 feature races. He famously once said, "Floyd could drive a dump truck."

Pat Patrick

Another of Floyd's biggest rivals but also a friend, Ohio's Pat Patrick finished a stellar career with more than 500 feature race wins across Ohio, Kentucky, Indiana, and West Virginia. Pat began in the 1960s and was winning races well into the late 1980s, successfully making the transition from heavy, homebuilt steel-bodied cars to the lightweight, small-block cars that replaced them. Twice runner-up in the World 100, he was inducted into the National Dirt Late Model Hall of Fame in 2002.

Gene Petro

Among Floyd's closest racing friends was Indiana native Gene Petro, who amassed more than 400 feature race wins across the Midwest tracks in Illinois, Indiana, Ohio, Kentucky, and Florida, where he relocated in the mid-1970s. Besides fielding his own cars, Petro enjoyed success driving for Lloyd Ruth and Morgan Chandler, among others. He was inducted into the National Dirt Late Model Hall of Fame in 2007.

E.M. Snowden Jr.

Regarded as among the best of the Bluegrass state racers, Snowden entered the fray with a homebuilt Camaro and was always tough to beat, especially on the bullrings like Richmond and Ponderosa (where he won track championships) and Taylor County. He later drove and won races for R.L. Duncan but was best known for fielding his own cars. One of the era's cleanest racers, Snowden unofficially won more than 100 feature races.

David Speer

Billy Teegarden once called David Speer the greatest qualifier he'd ever seen, and that is saying something. Speer collected more than 250 feature wins during a career that included stints driving for car owners R.L. Duncan, Bobby Paul and Dale Napper. The Kentucky native won big in his home state, and traveled for wins in Ohio, West Virginia, Tennessee, and Florida. He completed for a time in the NDRA. Speer was inducted into the National Dirt Late Model Hall of Fame in 2007.

Charlie Swartz

One of the great innovators in dirt late model racing, Charlie Swartz progressed from the steel-bodied 8-Ball Chevelle of the early 1970s to the lighter cars, then to constructing his own chassis designs. The second-generation driver is a former winner of the World 100 and the World Dirt Track Championship, as well as more than 500 feature races in both late models and sprint cars. He successfully competed in many touring series and was a first ballot selection for the National Dirt Late Model Hall of Fame in 2001.

Billy Teegarden

Nobody's career is more intertwined with Floyd Gilbert's than Billy Teegarden's. From wrestling for track titles at Tri-County, Glen Este, and Northern Kentucky, to being temporary teammates chasing each other, to the embattled 1973 split with Morgan Chandler, to Teegarden finishing behind Floyd at the 1973 World 100, the two will be forever linked. A great racer with 400 feature wins, Teegarden later manufactured the Dazzler chassis and

Hall of Fame driver Billy Teegarden was among Gilbert's toughest rivals, a former teammate and the man who chased him to the checkers at the World 100. (Courtesy Fremont Speedway Hall of Fame, Mid-American Auto Racing News Archives)

promoted a race track. He followed Gilbert into the National Dirt Late Model Hall of Fame in 2005.

Paul "Butterball" Woodridge

Kentucky's most successful racer during the steel-bodied late model era of the 1970s, Wooldridge won more than 400 feature races and multiple track titles at places like Richmond, Taylor County, and Franklin County. His epic battles with Gilbert during the early 1970s are legendary, with Wooldridge winning many of the big money showdowns in the R.L. Duncan Chevelle. Wooldridge was inducted into the National Dirt Late Model Hall of Fame in 2008, and the Kentucky Motorsports Hall of Fame in 2011.

Floyd Gilbert (left) clowns around trying to steal Paul "Butterball" Wooldridge's cigar after he drove Gilbert's No. 11 Chevelle to victory over Gilbert at Clay City Raceway in 1971. (Courtesy Fremont Speedway Hall of Fame, Mid-American Auto Racing News Archives)

CHAPTER 15:

Secrets of Success

It takes a special breed to hurtle headlong into a corner and know the exact instant to throw a race car into a broad slide, feather then mash the throttle, and have enough control to ride on the ragged edge. Fewer still are those who can accomplish those maneuvers lap after lap while keeping one eye on the competition and another on the ever-changing racing surface, interpreting the sensations coming from the race car the entire time. It is fighter pilot intense, and far harder than it looks. Great race car drivers have an abundance of confidence: not false, boisterous bravado, but the inner strength to know their skillset is as good or better than the competition.

"When I went to the track, and they would ask me, 'Who is going to win tonight?' I would say 'I didn't come here to run second.' After a while, I had the confidence," Floyd told DirtFans.com. "This is why I would shy away from a lot. Fact is, most of the time when I won a race, I would get my money, then leave. I just tried not to make anybody think my head was big by bragging after the win."

We can attribute that confidence to his humble beginnings and years of struggling to have competitive equipment.

"It's been a hard grind, getting up to something decent as far as equipment is concerned," he told the *Cincinnati Enquirer* in 1971. "But I did it with my own two hands. I've worked for it all. I don't knock

117

anyone in racing. It's my living, and I'll try the best I can to help racing. It's a hard game, but it's a lot of fun."

Gilbert, shown here holding the trophy for one of his Glen Este Speedway championships, was skillful, determined and a master of reading track surfaces. (Courtesy Fremont Speedway Hall of Fame, Mid-American Auto Racing News Archives)

Gilbert claims determination was his greatest strength as a driver.

"I was determined that I was going to get as good as anyone could get. I would really shy away from all the hullabaloo stuff. I didn't want anyone to think my head was as big as a watermelon," Floyd said. "I always said if you can make a car turn in twenty seconds, then I can do it in nineteen seconds, whether or not I did. That was my mindset."

How's this for determination? Larry Moore recounted the time Gilbert repaired a leaking tire during the race.

"One time at Florence, Floyd had this big old seventeen-inch-wide rear tire that we used to use on these big old steel wheels before aluminum. He had tubes in his, and he had run into somebody with the right rear," Moore recounted. "Well, there was a red flag, and at Florence under red, you could work on your car. He got a sledgehammer and was pushing a tube in the right rear wheel. It caught the bead and was sticking out. He had a guy helping him hold a screwdriver, and he beat that wheel in and then he won the race."

Did Gilbert think he had a weakness? No. Another key, he said, was maintaining his cool.

"I learned early on coming up in racing to be very, uh...don't get uptight. You know, be very calm; no matter what, be very calm. And that worked. I found after I learned how to do that, racing was easy," Floyd said. "If you're going to be uptight driving a race car, you're going to screw up. I hit the wall many times. Hit the inside wall, outside wall, I've rolled over, and had as much fun as anybody."

Indiana's Tom Helfrich, a 2002 inductee into the National Dirt Late Model Hall of Fame, towed to Kentucky nearly every week in the mid-1970s just to race with drivers like Gilbert and Pat Patrick, whom he considered the best of that era.

"He [Gilbert] was just good. He was good at all kinds of tracks. No matter what the track condition was. When the tracks got really slippery, or you couldn't flat out run with the foot on the floor, he seemed to shine a bit more in those kinds of conditions," Helfrich said in a 2018 interview. "He had a good feel for a car. You hardly ever saw him in trouble or out of shape. He was kind of my idol—him and Pat Patrick."

To that point, Gilbert confessed to DirtFans.com that throttle control was a big part of his game, saying, "I was the greatest feather foot there ever was. I could just about always pick where I wanted to turn, and I would always be a little slower than everyone else. But boy, when it was time to go, my engine lit up."

Having great equipment was certainly an advantage. In its July 2013 edition, *Late Model Illustrated* magazine chronicled some of the "most dominating cars in dirt late model history," a collection assembled by Hall of Fame historian Bob Markos. There on pages 61-62 were both Morgan Chandler's No. 28 Chevelle and the No. 59 Duncan's Delight Chevelle.

Larry Moore called Gilbert the most unique character he'd ever met in racing. Writing in his autobiography *On Top of the World; The Life and Times of a Racing Pioneer*, Moore called Floyd talented, sly, and a smart racer. "He was short, bow-legged, and was built like a rock," Moore wrote.

He also related how Gilbert taught him to read tires without a tire gauge.

"Them things lie to you," Gilbert told Moore about tire gauges. "So, he would either kick the tire with his foot or use his hand to feel it, because he insisted that was more reliable. And believe it or not, he taught me how to feel the difference in air pressure with my hand. It's a fact; you can actually feel the difference between ten and twelve pounds, for example," Moore wrote in his autobiography. "That proved to be helpful, because before the race I could slip around to other cars and feel their tires and know what pressure they were running. That's a true story."

Longtime rival and fellow Hall of Famer Billy Teegarden offered a somewhat different take on Floyd.

"Now that ... Floyd, he was somewhat of a horse's ass, but he belongs in the Hall of Fame," the outspoken Teegarden told DirtFans.com. "I mean, he was an *arrogant* bastard. He would tell you he was going to beat you, and if you wasn't damn careful, he'd do it. And I mean they ain't nobody that knows that SOB. We done a lot of racing together, and I know him about as well as anybody—and that SOB is insane ... I seen the SOB sit in the qualifying line with a handkerchief and blindfold himself. Wouldn't look at nobody or nothing clear up until he got ready to go out on the racetrack and pull that blindfold off and go out there and set on the pole."

What Floyd apparently never told Billy was his actions had more to do with track conditions and less with getting psyched up.

"As many years as I was in, it kind of helped, having a photographic mind; I did in a sense," Floyd told DirtFans.com. "I could look at a track and tell by the color what the car would do on it. One thing about it, I knew dirt and I knew it by its color. You start out in the early evening and the track is dark, it was wet and damp. So, I would wait and qualify when the track was a certain color."

In his dominant 1972 Clay City campaign, winning ten of eleven features, Gilbert was most often the first driver out to qualify because he knew that track would typically dry out and lose grip as the night wore on. That wasn't the case at Florence, or what was then called Northern Kentucky Speedway.

"Over at Northern Kentucky, they got to where nobody would qualify until after I did. I sat in the infield one night. The track was wet, and nobody would go out. So, I went out in the infield thinking I might drag some of them out. But nobody came out. And someone at the track there got mad at me. I told them, 'You give me another lap later, and I'll go on.' He said, 'I can't do that.' I said, 'Well then, I'm going to sit here until that track gets the color I want it.' And I did," he recalled.

In a *Dirt Late Model* magazine profile entitled "Floyd Gilbert, World Class Racer," writer J.T. LeFever offered, "Floyd Gilbert is one of the most revered and successful drivers of the Central Kentucky/Southern Ohio/Indiana region, as well as the early period of dirt late model racing." LeFever likened Floyd to Hall of Famer Scott Bloomquist for the way he would psych out the competition, and how he used interviews at the track and in the media to promote a love or hate relationship with fans.

Longtime Gilbert friend and former crew member Mike Roland called Floyd one of the most intelligent drivers he'd ever met.

"It took a lot to know Floyd, even just a little bit," Roland said. "Floyd was kind of to himself. He was the type of driver that would psych himself up before a race. He would get to the track early in the day. It didn't matter where it was at, Floyd was there early.

"Floyd was so concentrated on his racing. I've seen him just walk around the race track and study it. He would psych himself up, saying, 'I am the greatest. I know this track, I'm going to win.' That's an old story from Billy Teegarden about Floyd, but I saw him do that," Roland said. "Floyd was very hard-nosed."

And superstitious, according to LeFever.

"He would pull off at this little roadside park on the way to Northern Kentucky Speedway at nine or ten o'clock in the morning. If he went somewhere and won, he did that same routine every week from then on. We would go early ,and he'd be sitting there at that little park," LeFever said.

Late model driver Roger Grossnickle recalls the first time he ever raced against Gilbert on a spring Sunday afternoon at Eldora Speedway.

"It was so dusty that you could not see. I could see the light poles, but that was the only way I could see going down the backstretch. And Floyd went around everybody and lapped the whole field," Grossnickle recalled. "How could he do that? Nobody was passing. I wound up fifth my first time at Eldora."

A friend of Grossnickle approached Gilbert the following week to ask him about that day.

"Floyd, the first time we run against you, you lapped us and we'd never been lapped. What is your secret?" the man asked.

"Well, you know most race car drivers, when conditions get like that and the track gets dusty, will close one eye and then close the other one?"

"Yes," the man hesitantly replied. "Well, old Floyd just closes 'em both and goes on," Gilbert said.

"Floyd looked straight ahead, never looked at the guy, just as calm as can be," Grossnickle said.

Sometimes it may have been easier than it appeared, according to J.T. LeFever.

"Floyd, Vern, and Dick DeBolt got together one night and put the top three money together and drew straws. However, their straws came up is how they would finish, but they agreed everybody would lead during the feature," LeFever said. "So, they all three led. Floyd won, my dad was second, and DeBolt was third. And they all finished the way they were supposed to finish, but they all laughed because everybody got the same money."

Bubby James ran fifth that night and found out what had happened.

"That's not fair; nobody asked me," an irritated James told Vern LeFevers, who replied, "We didn't figure you had a shot at winning. We were playing around, and [evidently] you didn't."

Gilbert said he had some basic criteria for the tracks where he ran.

"There wasn't many tracks I didn't like. If I didn't like it, I wouldn't go," he told DirtFans.com "And if they wouldn't let me drink my beer,

I wouldn't stay. Me and (Gene) Petro, we liked to drink our beer. Never caused trouble, never drank it out in the open. Generally went to the motorhome. Hardly ever watched another race I wasn't in. I might watch a little bit to see how the track was and how the cars were handling."

In his interview with Floyd., J.T. LeFever told a personal story.

"When I was a little kid, I was playing at Northern Kentucky Speedway and you walked by on your way to the pits. I can remember tugging on your uniform as you passed by. I'll never forget you stopping and talking to me just like I was a big person, and taking time out for me," LeFever told Floyd, who typically paid attention to younger fans.

"I learned early on to take care of the kids. They'll bring momma and papa back," Floyd said. "I was signing autographs in Whitewater Valley Speedway's grandstands, and they were lining up the race. They were yelling 'Come on, Floyd, get in the car.' I said, 'Now, wait a minute, these kids are first.' I signed about a dozen more and went and got in the car and beat Pat Patrick by about a half a car that night."

More than just a fan favorite, Floyd Gilbert was a hero to young fans. Here he is surrounded by youngsters after winning a 1972 feature at Clay City Raceway. The author, then age 14, stands at far right. (Photo by Steve Cottle, courtesy author's collection.

Another example of his connection to younger fans is a victory lane photo from Clay City Raceway during Floyd's remarkable 1972 season. In the August 11 image, which was published many times in *Mid-American Auto Racing News*, photographer Steve Cottle captured Floyd with the checkered flag—but the Morgan Chandler Chevelle was all but invisible, because he was surrounded by seventeen youngsters, ranging from elementary school to junior high school age.

Flyin' Floyd poses beside a No. 1 Chevelle renumbered 11 with duct tape at Eldora Speedway. This car was owned by John and Alan Miller. (Photo by Ray Rogers, from Nelson Wierenga collection, courtesy Bob Markos)

Another image from Eldora Speedway shows Floyd in line and ready to qualify behind the wheel of this No. 21 Camaro. (Photo by Ray Rogers, from Nelson Wierenga collection, courtesy Bob Markos)

"I've had my ups and down," Floyd told DirtFans.com with great candor. "Been a lot of ups and a lot of downs. I went down the drain as much as anybody's had a chance at going down the drain, but yet I was strong enough to pull myself back out of it. And been a few times in life I just sit and bawled 'cause things just haven't went right."

Floyd described himself as "an unusual person with an unusual life."

In the 1975 SCR feature, Gilbert praised his wife, saying "Anyone who put up with me for twenty-five years deserves more than I can give her."

He offered a strong assessment in the DirtFans interview.

"I mean, we didn't hardly have bread in the house. If it hadn't been for [Floyd's wife] Dee making forty dollars a week, I wouldn't have been able to do it. I have to give her credit," he said. "I had my motorhome; I got in it and I drank my beer, and never worried about whether someone was going to beat me or if I'm going to beat them," he said. "My words were, 'I didn't come to the track to run second,' and that's the way I felt."

Track Championships:

Bluestone Speedway 1971, 1974
Brown County Speedway 1976
Clay City Raceway 1971, 1972
Glen Este Speedway 1961, 1970, 1971, 1972, 1973
Northern Kentucky Speedway 1976
Ponderosa Speedway 1972, 1974
Whitewater Valley Speedway 1970, 1972

CHAPTER 16:

Hall of Fame Beckons

Many of Floyd Gilbert's most memorable victories occurred at Northern Kentucky Speedway, since rebranded Florence Speedway, just a short haul from his Ohio home. He returned there in the summer of 2004. Not to wheel a late model, although few doubted he still could, but for something far more lasting: his induction into the National Dirt Late Model Hall of Fame.

Today, Floyd's presence there includes an array of photographs, a copy of the J.T. LeFever story from *Dirt Late Model* magazine, a door from the No. 12 Camaro he raced in 1975, and the trophy from the 1973 Johnny Appleseed 150.

Floyd Gilbert (center) speaks during Gilbert's 2004 induction into the National Dirt Late Model Hall of Fame. He is flanked by announcer James Essex (left) and legendary racing journalist Chris Economacki. (Author's collection)

Entering the Hall of Fame was more than a physical homecoming. Enshrined in the three classes before him were former rivals Rodney Combs, Larry Moore, and Charlie Swartz in 2001; Tom Helfrich, Pat Patrick, and Bob Wearing in 2002; and Delmas Conley, Jim Curry, Ray Godsey, and Russ Petro in 2003. Some might rightfully characterize Floyd's induction as overdue. Vern LeFevers thought so, lobbying for his former rival to go in before him.

Among those who would follow Floyd into the National Dirt Late Model Hall of Fame in subsequent years were Billy Teegarden, Ralph Latham, Vern LeFevers, Gene Petro, David Speer, Chuck McWilliams, Butterball Wooldridge, Morgan Chandler, Bruce Gould, Fats Coffey, and Eddie Carrier Sr.

Sporting a plaid shirt, suspenders, jeans, blue Valley Radiator hat, and his trademark dark sunglasses, Gilbert—whose beard and hair had turned gray—took his spot on the flatbed trailer which doubled as a stage in the track infield next to Iowan Ed Sanger, another former World 100 winner, in the hall's fourth class. It was a worthy group, including five-time USAC stock car champ Butch Hartman, Tennessee's Ronnie Johnson, Pennsylvania's Chub Frank, Virginia's Rodney Franklin, and Kentucky car owner and sponsor Bob Miller.

Host James Essex hailed Floyd as one of the real icons of dirt track racing, and briefly recited some career highlights:

- Started in 1951 at Glen Este Speedway near Cincinnati.
- Raced extensively across Kentucky, Ohio and Indiana.
- Enjoyed a decade of legendary battles against many others already or soon to be enshrined.
- Became a full-time race driver in 1970, which included racing every winter in the southeast.
- His 1971 streak of 21 consecutive wins over seven weekends at three different tracks.
- His iconic 42 wins at age 42 driving Morgan Chandler's Chevelle to four track championships.
- Moving to the R.L. Duncan team in 1973 and winning the World 100 at Eldora Speedway.

- Being named 1973 Mid-American Auto Racing News Driver of the Year.
- Sixteen total track championships and 500-plus wins—statistics comparable to those posted by Ed Sanger and Chub Frank as most among that season's class.

"I would like to thank Morgan Chandler and Cecil Snell and the crew of twenty-eight; Lloyd Ruth [29] and Earl Rogers and crew of twenty-two; Bob Busener, who helped me get away from the junkers; R.L. Duncan of fifty-nine; Charles and Logan Grider; John Holmes at Valley Radiator, who really was one of the great people. The fans that really rooted for me. My wife and kids that put up with me," a stoic Gilbert said during his brief acceptance speech.

Chris Economacki, legendary broadcaster and founder of National Speed Sport News then spoke briefly and complimented Floyd because his last name was only seven letters, so it was easy to fit into a headline, especially compared to John Mugavin—which, ironically, also has seven letters. Economacki then conducted a brief interview, asking Gilbert, "Who was the toughest driver you ever came up against on the track?"

"Local in Cincinnati, I would say to pick just one, that is hard to say," Floyd responded. "Vern LeFevers was really tough. I hated to see him at a track, because one of us was going to win."

Economacki chided Floyd, saying, "But one of you was going to lose." Floyd replied, "I wanted to win."

ABOUT THE AUTHOR

DAVID M. MCGEE is an award-winning writer, journalist, and racing historian. He serves as the senior public address announcer at Bristol Motor Speedway, special events announcer at Bristol Dragway, and historian for both facilities.

He has 40-plus years in motorsports and is the author of six previous books on racing history, including four dealing with Bristol; the latest being BRISTOL: *Stories of Oval and Drag Racing in Thunder Valley* from CarTech Publishing.

He is a news reporter for the *Bristol Herald Courier* newspaper where he helped win the 2018 Scripps Howard Award for Community Journalism and a wide range of national, state, and regional press awards.

McGee is actively involved in preserving the racing history of East Tennessee, Eastern and Central Kentucky and Southwest Virginia—areas rich in heritage but too often overlooked for their contributions.

He is a voting member for the National Dirt Late Model Hall of Fame and Kentucky Motorsports Hall of Fame, in his native Kentucky. He is a graduate of Morehead State University.

Find him at davidmcgeeauthor.wordpress.com or visit www.facebook.com/DavidMcGeeAuthor.

INDEX

Printed in the USA
CPSIA information can be obtained
at www.ICGtesting.com
LVHW020744240823
756131LV00006B/75